CHALLENGES
OF THE
NARROW WAY

Text copyright © Bridget Plass 2004
The author asserts the moral right
to be identified as the author of this work

Published by
The Bible Reading Fellowship
First Floor, Elsfield Hall
15–17 Elsfield Way, Oxford OX2 8FG

ISBN 1 84101 365 X
First published 2004
10 9 8 7 6 5 4 3 2 1 0
All rights reserved

Acknowledgments
Unless otherwise stated, scripture quotations are taken from the Contemporary
English Version of the Bible published by HarperCollins Publishers, copyright ©
1991, 1992, 1995 American Bible Society.

Scripture quotations taken from the *Holy Bible, New International Version*, copyright
© 1973, 1978, 1984 by International Bible Society. Used by permission of
Hodder & Stoughton Limited. All rights reserved. 'NIV' is a registered trademark
of International Bible Society. UK trademark number 1448790.

Scripture quotations from The New Revised Standard Version of the Bible,
Anglicized Edition, copyright © 1989, 1995 by the Division of Christian
Education of the National Council of the Churches of Christ in the United States
of America, are used by permission. All rights reserved.

Scripture quotations from the Good News Bible, published by The Bible
Societies/HarperCollins Publishers, copyright © 1966, 1971, 1976, 1992
American Bible Society, are used by permission.

Every effort has been made to contact copyright owners for the poems in this
book. If further information is received, full credit will be given in case of reprint.

A catalogue record for this book is available from the British Library

Printed and bound in Great Britain by
Bookmarque, Croydon

CONTENTS

The life that halts short of the cross is but a fugitive and condemned thing, doomed at last to be lost beyond recovery. That life which goes to the cross and loses itself there to rise again with Christ is a divine and deathless treasure... The man who takes his cross and follows Christ will soon find that his direction is away from the sepulchre. Death is behind him and a joyous and increasing life before.

A.J. TOZER, THE DIVINE CONQUEST

THE DECISION TO FOLLOW

(and why we don't!)

He who would valiant be, let him come hither
Well, yes—quite
Absolutely
Let him come!
I'll be along in a minute
Not that I'm against hithering, you understand
I'm a hitherer
I am a hithering person—definitely am a potential one.
It's just that—well, I've had to put the old hithering on hold for a bit
I suppose you could say I'm in the Slough of thing
Thingy
Things
The Slough of things
Couple of friendly bombs probably do the trick.
Hmmm…
First avowed intent still intact, mind you
Oh, yes, to be—a proper one
To be a pilgrim…

. . . .

Tell me, do your fancies seem to flee away?
Mine don't
Large, lazy, flightless birds, my fancies—like emus
They just run and run and run and run…
Do you know, I really rather fear what men say
I suppose
The long and the short of it is—I do labour night and day
In a way
But I'm not sure I've even begun
To be a pilgrim.

ADRIAN PLASS

(FROM *NEVER MIND THE REVERSING DUCKS*)

GATES AND WAYS

'I am the way, the truth, and the life!' Jesus answered. 'Without me, no one can go to the Father... Have faith in me when I say that the Father is one with me and that I am one with the Father. Or else have faith in me simply because of the things I do... I cannot speak with you much longer, because the ruler of this world is coming. But he has no power over me. I obey my Father, so that everyone in the world might know that I love him. It is time for us to go now.'

JOHN 14:6, 11, 30–31

God can be trusted not to let you be tempted too much, and he will show you how to escape from your temptations.

1 CORINTHIANS 10:13

From the point when Jesus decided the time had come to make his way to Jerusalem, knowing that when he got there he would be arrested, tried and murdered, he began to teach in an increasingly fervent and direct way. Presumably he was fuelled by a sense of increasing urgency. Maybe he felt he could no longer afford the luxury of allowing his followers to chew over and variously interpret his colourful stories. Whatever the reason, we find him spelling out what is to happen to him in no uncertain terms and stating more clearly than ever his relationship to the Father and the vital importance of his role as 'the way, the truth, and the life'.

He emphasizes again and again the need to follow him, whatever that will mean in terms of cost, and he makes no bones about the level of commitment that will be required. He talks of the dangers of worrying, of storing up riches, and of avoiding the call to go through the narrow door.

The narrow door—or 'gate' as it is sometimes called.

I wonder if any of you felt the same shiver of fear that I did as a child on looking at Tenniel's illustrations of the grotesquely enlarged Alice trapped in the little crooked Wonderland house where doors and windows and fellow creatures were minute by comparison. Fortunately, an equally vivid image from my childhood is that of the door in Frances Hodgson Burnett's magical story, the one that had been kept locked for many years but, on being opened, revealed a mysterious secret garden that would become beautiful with loving care.

The narrow gate is like this. On the one hand, it is a fearful thing that few will manage to enter. On the other, it is the entrance to a life never before dreamed of once the key is discovered.

A real problem for those of us who are trying to follow Jesus in the 21st century is that it is difficult for us to appreciate his image of 'gates'. We associate them with the small wooden things that creak a little when we push them open on our way up to our neat front doors. None of us lives in a walled city where the only way in is through a gate. Narrow gates represented safety to the contemporaries of Jesus: they could keep marauding hordes at bay. Perhaps, for us, the image of the turnstiles at football grounds might be a more appropriate, if less visually pleasing, analogy. The Jews naturally assumed that heaven and hell also had gates, usually with guards posted to fend off those who were unwelcome visitors—and of course the image of the 'pearly gates' remains with us to this day.

We have similar difficulty accessing the image Jesus gave of himself as the gate to the sheepfold (John 10:7). Contrary to anything we may have gleaned from TV programmes such as *One Man and His Dog*, sheepfolds didn't have gates at the time of Jesus. The shepherd himself would seal the entrance to the fold by lying down in front of it, thus protecting his flock from wild animals and thieves. Jesus' listeners would have understood. He was saying that everyone seeking to enter God's kingdom must do so over his live body and that once they have entered they will be safe from enemy attack.

Biblical references to 'the way' might have some significance for the ramblers among us but tend to leave most of us a bit cold. We do not have to journey on foot from place to place following rough tracks, where staying safe is a major priority and where losing one's way could mean the difference between life and death. We lack the Jewish tradition of God's truth being a path that can be found and followed. The image is merely allegorical now, but does this mean that the concepts are irrelevant? Of course not. Our speech is littered with expressions such as 'keeping on the straight and narrow', 'falling by the wayside' and being 'led astray' by 'wolves in sheep's clothing'. Indeed, the concept of life as a journey is increasingly popular, while one of the most popular phrases bandied about in 'Christianese' has God 'opening and closing doors' as though he spends most of his time as a glorified doorman.

The truth is that nothing has really changed. Following the Way and entering the gate (or door) still attract us and frighten us in equal proportions. We still talk about it rather than doing it. We still struggle and get tangled up, and give up and turn back and then wish we hadn't!

Naturally, living in the West, we don't have camels either, but Jesus' picture of the eye of a needle being too narrow for a camel to pass through is still a graphic image (Matthew 19:24). If Jesus were here now, though, he would make his point using different illustrations, more familiar to us.

Take cats!

For years our family has had cats. They have varied from highly intelligent, sleek feline beauties to the fat and thick variety, but one thing they all have in common is whiskers. Why? Well, did you know that the span of a cat's whiskers is exactly the same as the widest part of its body? A cat can use its whiskers to test the width of a gap—ensuring that, even in the dark, the cat will not get stuck trying to squeeze through spaces too narrow for it. In the same way, as Paul assured the Corinthians, God does not wish us to be tempted beyond our capabilities to resist.

This Lent, we are going to set out on our own journey to try to discover truthfully where we are, how far we've come, what we want, and how (if we've got lost or given up) we can start again. The great news for us is that we can do this bearing in mind the words of Jesus. The Jesus who said 'I am the Way' will draw us to him and hold on to us throughout this time of discovery, however far we have fallen and however dangerous the terrain. Not only that, but we can believe Paul when he says that the Creator who saw fit to equip cats with their own safety measure will never force us to go through any gate too narrow for us until we have slimmed down sufficiently to enter.

❖

Dear Father, we want to use this time to examine truthfully our journey with you so far. We want to face the challenges that this will present and we want to face them head on. We want to be brave. We want to enter through the narrow gate and follow you on the way, however costly that might turn out to be, practically or emotionally.

AGREEING TO GO

Jesus replied, 'Those who love their lives will lose them, while those who hate their lives in this world will keep them for eternal life. Whoever serves me must follow me; and where I am, my servant also will be. My Father will honour the one who serves me.'

JOHN 12:25–26 (NIV)

Above our fireplace we have a mirror—a very special mirror. It was made for us by a very special man. One of life's heroes, in fact. A man who at a certain moment in his life showed immense courage and determination. A man with divinely royal connections. A man we are very proud to be associated with, although we hardly know him. We name-drop when we can. Sometimes in the evening when I am sitting on my own, I look at our mirror made of four rough panels from a 200-year-old church fence and beautifully adorned with twigs and small fir cones and tiny artificial butterflies, and I wish I could be as brave and honest as the creator of my mirror. So who is he?

Well, his name is Guz. On one particular day when he was 35 he made a courageous decision to walk away from the drugs and alcohol that were devastating his life and walk through the narrowest of doors towards freedom. It was a terrifying time. The way ahead looked sterile and dreary, with a gaping vacuum that could never again be filled by the cosy familiarity of his old friends, alcohol or drugs. It was going to be a long and lonely road with no escape exits, but he knew it was a black-and-white decision between life or certain death. He joined a residential recovery programme in Kent called the Kenward Trust. There he met Jesus, who became King and Lord of his life. With the help of staff, inmates and a local church, he managed to gain control of his life and set off in a new direction. At the time of writing, Guz is living with friends of ours, Margaret and Roy, who are wardens of a house where the men have considerable freedom to pursue a career again, renew relationships with family (where that is still possible) and look towards leaving the programme altogether and battling on along the way alone.

I was talking to Margaret a while ago and asked her what she most wanted for the men who come through the programme. She said, 'I want them to know what it is like to have life and to have it in abundance.' Those are the very words of our Lord, words intended for all of us: 'I came that they may have life, and have it abundantly' (John 10:10, NRSV).

Somehow it is difficult for those of us whose lives are not obviously in shreds to see entering the narrow door as a decision between life and death, and yet that is exactly what Jesus is saying. He makes no bones about it. Only if we are prepared to follow him through the door and along the narrow way will we have the extraordinary privilege of being able to live for eternity in heaven with him.

If it is so straightforward, why aren't we jamming the narrow gate to get through? Some of us think nothing of queuing all night in the street to be among the first to rush through a shop door for a sales bargain, or outside the foyer of a theatre to get into a concert. On the other side of this particular door, we are told, we will find life in abundance—life with the Jesus who loved us enough to die for us, life with the Father who created us and loves us so much. It seems so obvious, so clear.

The hard truth we have to face is that many of us are addicts, or on the way to becoming addicts. Like the rich young man in Matthew 19:16–22, we are addicted to and dependent on our escapist world, on comforts that have become essential props to help us function day by day. We cannot visualize coping without them. We are in danger of losing our lives because of our love of trivial pursuits and, like all addicts, our vision becomes increasingly distorted.

Many addicts convince themselves for years that they can stop doing what they do if they so choose—that it doesn't have a hold over them, that they could walk away from it with ease if they wanted. We equally convince ourselves that we could give up anything and everything and follow him if we chose.

'I like TV as much as the next person but I don't have to watch it. I mean, I'm not hooked. OK, so up till now I probably have watched it most evenings but I don't need to.'

'Yes, I do like to know there's a bit of money put by for a rainy day, but if I felt God wanted it, well of course I…'

The problem is that addiction creeps up slowly and insidiously. In the case of gambling, alcoholism or drugs, the effects are obvious, the fall-out evident. The grip comfort has on us is more subtle. It doesn't cause family breakdown or bankruptcy. It merely slows us down, takes the edge off our decision-making powers and dulls our responses. It's not that Jesus is no longer there, still calling us, still waiting for us. It's just that it all seems so much effort actually to get up out of our armchairs.

'Anyway, the time doesn't feel quite right yet—I mean, he hasn't actually asked me to…' turns into 'Surely at my age he wouldn't expect…' so gradually that we hardly notice it.

'And… well, I'd always understood it's up to us, isn't it?'

Well, yes it is. It always was. We have always had the option to sit stubbornly on this side of the narrow door, hanging on to our way of life for grim death—or until grim death.

There has always been another choice—the choice made by Guz and hundreds like him, which is to have the courage and honesty to acknowledge our areas of addiction, accept our frailty and take the hand of the only one who can lead us through the door that separates life from death.

❖

Dear Father, forgive us for the many times when we have refused your invitation to the party because we are too busy and too distracted by the world to see clearly what our priorities need to be. Help us to identify what is holding us in its grip and rescue us, we beg you, dear Father.

AFRAID OF WHAT OTHERS MIGHT SAY

Even then, many of the leaders put their faith in Jesus, but they did not tell anyone about it. The Pharisees had already given orders for the people not to have anything to do with anyone who had faith in Jesus. And besides, the leaders liked praise from others more than they liked praise from God.

JOHN 12:42–43

We meet cosily every Sunday to pore over the glossy travel brochures full of pictures of wild, beautiful, far-off locations and talk about how much we'd love to go on an expedition to such places. Some of us pretend we've been there and share tales of what we experienced. Some of us go to huge meetings to hear more about how important it is that we make such an expedition, and while we are there we equip ourselves with every possible bit of travel equipment and buy piles of guidebooks.

Most of us know that deep down we have no intention of going anywhere, even if keeping up the pretence is costly in terms of time and energy and even money, and means we are plumping for a half-life and opting for a lukewarm, sentimental relationship with Jesus. Why?

Could it be because we are afraid—terrified of plunging into the unknown, of being in unfamiliar territory without a map? Above all, most of us hate change. Change threatens our security and undermines our confidence. It affects our familiar role in our social group. It can make us feel as useless and helpless as experiencing an emergency in a foreign country where you cannot speak the language.

Perhaps more than any other aspect of change, we fear what others will say of us if we attempt to leave base camp.

We live on the south coast and, high on the cliffs overlooking Eastbourne, you can experience a phenomenon reserved for exposed, windswept areas. Sometimes it is incredibly hard to keep your balance; your hair feels as if it is being tugged out by the roots and your legs are in danger of giving way. You descend from the hills feeling as if you have been pummelled into a new shape. The scenery up there shows similar signs of the strength of wind power. Not one of the trees and bushes has reached its potential and grown straight and beautiful and tall. They have all been stunted and bent over like little old ladies by the strong prevailing coastal winds.

And so it is with many of us. I know the phenomenon all too well. For much of my young life, I felt as though somewhere out there was a strong prevailing wind forcing me to adopt an ugly distorted shape in order to survive. I think it started when I was eleven and transferred from a small convent junior school to a much bigger and tougher secondary school. I didn't speak right. I didn't understand the jokes. I felt like an alien and I felt confused. What was wrong with me? I began a long, costly period of trying to fit in. At school I spoke with as strong a local accent as I could, laughed hysterically at jokes I didn't understand, became obsessed by the way I looked, aped every extreme fashion style, tried to work out how to get detention and by 16 had become anorexic and isolated. It was only when I went into the sixth form and dis-covered a bully-free environment that my equilibrium and my health, both mental and physical, began to be restored… only to be shaken again when I went to university.

Being a drama student at university in the 1960s was a challenge to sanity. At a time when 'anything went', being boring was the ultimate crime and everyone was terrified of missing the next Dylanesque legend about to burst on to the scene. As being stoned was considered a requisite for any genuine creativity, most of the class's dramatic offerings were bizarre, to say the least. Having promised my mum I wouldn't take drugs, I was like the child looking at the emperor's new clothes most of the time, but became expert again at aping the prevailing fashion—greeting with joyous cries of acclamation the most inept art and dramatic writing. So extreme was the position I had to adopt that even I could see it was ludicrous. This was a good thing as it meant that God was at last able to get a small word in edgewise, and I began the slow and painful stretching exercises needed to get myself back to the comfortable position that God intended for me.

We are all shaped by the prevailing winds of fashionable behaviour, whether it is in church or in society. We all want to fit in as much as the ugly duckling in Hans Christian Andersen's fairy tale. None of us wants to be different. All of us fear being 'boring'. We reject the small, sane voice of common sense, contort our mental processes and tie ourselves in knots simply in order to fit in. It can involve some pretty ludicrous posturing. As David Persimmon, the lovable, irrascible and extremely unhappy vicar in Adrian Plass' *Alien at St Wilfred's*, says, 'I read *Private Eye* and *Renewal*. I hide *Renewal* in *Private Eye*, and *Private Eye* in *Renewal*, depending on who I'm with at the time.'

Acknowleging the possibility that God may be calling us out of the pack and asking us to set off alone is seriously threatening. What will be demanded of us? Will we have to be 'holy'? Will we have to give up some of the social activities that, up until now, we may have occasionally acknowledged to be a bit debatable but not worried about unduly? Will our church friends think us arrogant or wilful or deluded? Will they be cross with us? Look down on us? Not like us any more? Reject us?

The alternative is surely more frightening. Abundant life is not borne on the prevailing winds either in the church or in the world. In bending to those winds, we are in danger of never reaching our

God-given potential. We might even, as I did in my teens, put our mental, physical and spiritual health at risk.

❖

Dear Father, please help me. Give me the courage to withstand the cowardice that is within me. Give me the strength to push against the weight of the wind power of the world and the church and follow you.

THE NARROW WAY'S GOOD AND BAD PRESS

Jesus answered, 'Do all you can to go in by the narrow door! A lot of people will try to get in, but will not be able to.'

LUKE 13:23–24

There are, of course, many other reasons why we hesitate about making an all-out commitment to follow Jesus. One is the negative light in which the 'narrow gate' and the 'narrow way' are portrayed. Luke suggests a clamouring at the door from people who are desperate to get in, indicating something very exciting beyond, and we know from our hymns that we can 'walk with him and talk with him along life's narrow way'. So where does the bad press come from?

I suspect it to be one of the lies spun by wolves in sheep's clothing. The narrow way is represented as a list of 'shalt nots' by Pharisaical thinkers. Let's face it, being told we must 'keep to the straight and narrow' sounds stern, dry and sacrificial, not to say downright boring, and has a very debilitating effect on would-be pilgrims. We feel defeated before we start because we know we'll never be good enough to stay on it. We hear absolutely no hint whatsoever of walking with Jesus and talking with him.

This myth of exclusivity was encouraged by the Pharisees in Jesus' day and the equivalents in our own. For some Christians, the narrow way is something they are on but everyone else isn't! In our own town we have a denomination that describes itself as 'strict and particular'. Can you imagine a newcomer to the town looking to find the right place of worship for them and, seeing this inscription above the door, saying, 'Wow—now that's for me'? Yet at some point in history a group of people decided that that is what they wanted to be called.

For others, the concept of a narrow way seems at variance with what some of our lively evangelical churches are telling us.

In *The Divine Conquest*, A.J. Tozer wrote about what he called the 'new cross':

If I see aright, the cross of popular evangelism is not the cross of the New Testament. It is rather a new bright ornament upon the bosom of a self assured and carnal Christianity... The old cross slew men: the new cross entertains them.

He goes on to say:

I well know how many smooth arguments support the new cross. Does not the new cross win converts and make many followers and so carry the advantage of numerical success? Should we not adjust ourselves to changing times? Have we not heard the slogan, 'New days, new ways'? ... Who today is interested in a gloomy mysticism that would sentence its flesh to a cross and recommend self-effacing humility as a virtue actually to be practised by modern Christians? These are the arguments, along with many more flippant still, which are brought forward to give an appearance of wisdom to the hollow and meaningless cross of popular Christianity.

I have to say that this rings a lot of bells with me. There does seem to be a feeling that we can enjoy Resurrection Sunday every day and forget Good Friday altogether. Tozer firmly believed that such teaching is wrong. He set down what he saw as the clear way to following Christ. He wrote:

It is the way of death unto life. Always life stands just beyond death and beckons the man who is sick of himself to come and know the life more abundant… But to reach new life he must pass temporarily through the valley of the shadow of death.'

So in other words both extremes are wrong. The dreary, musty, solemn, subdued, miserable image is a gross parody of life in Christ, but so too is the concept that walking the Christian way should be like little Charlie finding a gold wrapper in a Willy Wonka chocolate bar, thus guaranteeing a gloriously trouble-free, chocolate-filled future.

Another problem is that, even if we wanted to, most of us are not sure how to go about entering the narrow way. We are not in the position in which Guz found himself, of having to choose between life and death, yet we know there is more to be experienced and sense that we have a decision to make before we can know what that greater experience is.

Adrian and I found ourselves in that position about 20 years ago. We had both in the past made a definite commitment to following Jesus but didn't feel we had made much progress at all. We had a family of three boys and belonged to a lively church where we were very involved in everything going on, but we were feeling increasingly frustrated. We felt we were becoming more and more like goldfish swimming around a safe little bowl. At the very least we wanted to get out into a small stream! So one evening, feeling a bit silly but at the same time acutely aware that what we were about to do was significant for us, we knelt down on the kitchen floor and said to God that we wanted him to take us and use us however he wanted and whatever that meant.

Four months later Adrian suffered a devastating breakdown! It didn't seem quite the answer we had anticipated. So much for the stream! We felt as though we had been thrown into rapids which we were unlikely to survive, but it was out of this that Adrian began to write, and I now feel that God took our words as seriously as we had tried to mean them.

※

Where do the readings of the last three days leave you? Have you ever taken the step of entering through the narrow gate?

Are you just too comfortable to get up and go? Have you settled for a lukewarm relationship with God because life is just too full and rich to bother looking for more?

Are you afraid?

Do you feel that your walk with God is a matter of life and death or more of a lifestyle choice? A privilege or a right? This could be time for you to take stock and ask him to show you where your relationship is growing cold and old.

Are you in fact struggling to say 'yes' to the adventure of following Jesus, even though you know it could be life-changing? Is this what your heart wants? This could be your opportunity to tell him.

CHILD ENOUGH TO FOLLOW MATURELY?

(Preparations for the journey)

I wish I was my son again
The first in all the world to know
The cornflake crisp of frosted grass
Beneath the polar paving stones,
Beneath the drip of liquid light
From watercolour winter suns.

ADRIAN PLASS

(FROM *CLEARING AWAY THE RUBBISH*)

READY FOR THE JOURNEY?

Once again Jesus spoke to the people. This time he said, 'I am the light for the world! Follow me, and you won't be walking in the dark. You will have the light that gives life.' ... Jesus answered, 'The light will be with you for only a little longer. Walk in the light while you can. Then you won't be caught walking blindly in the dark.'

JOHN 8:12; 12:35

Because of the excitement and confidence that so often accompany our first meeting with Jesus, it is easy to feel ready to agree to follow him to the ends of the world, whatever the cost and without preparation. For a while, that suffices. We can sing-along-a-Jesus without feeling that anything else is demanded of us. It is fun. It is exciting. It is safe.

But there came a time during Jesus' life on earth when he began to ask more of his followers. He began to give them more responsibilty, to lead them down paths that were no longer the equivalent of a Sunday afternoon stroll followed by tea and cakes. The way became narrower, the climbs more strenuous, the dangers more apparent. Paradoxically, they were challenged to abandon adult independence and become as dependent and as open to new experiences as a child. Only then, they were told, would they be able to enter the kingdom of God (Mark 10:15).

Still Jesus led the way until one day there came a point when he told his disciples that he was going on alone through the narrowest ravine of all, and he did not expect them to follow him there—not yet! They were not yet ready.

This week we are going to take time to examine what Jesus himself said about taking the serious step of following him wherever that might lead. We will think about the implications of leaving our safe camp where we know what to expect and where we know we will be happy and secure, to follow him wherever he leads us.

'I'm already well on the way,' might be your reasoned response. 'I've been following him for years.'

Fair enough, but here are two points to bear in mind. One: if you were starting again on your Christian life, what might you have done differently? What different or further preparations might you have made? The second point is: you never know what challenging new detours are waiting for you just round the corner, which will necessitate reviewing how equipped you are to cope.

When I was thinking about a theme for this book, I felt fairly comfortable with my choice. I had plenty of experiences to draw on from the past and felt reasonably confident that I knew a little of what I was talking about, having been a Christian for most of my life and having experienced and survived some pretty tough times on the way. I knew what it was like to feel lost and lonely, to be led astray, to climb what appeared to be a high mountain only to reach the summit and discover that it had been a mere hillock compared to the peaks that lay ahead. I felt that I had something to say about trusting God through crises and about his guidance. I also knew how it felt to sing in the rain and enjoy the sweet smells left after the storms had subsided.

Then, WHAM! It is true to say that throughout this entire time of writing, our immediate family has been buffeted by life storms such as we have never known before. The nearest I can come in describing how events have unfolded over the last 18 months is to draw an analogy with the television news bulletins. Stories that appear newsworthy in the morning have often been usurped by even more dramatic events by the evening. Some items, which on a calm day would have been the main story, never get higher than third or fourth on the list and sometimes disappear from the bottom and are never broadcast. Well, that is how it has felt for us.

It's not been a lot of fun, really—and there hasn't been much of a choice about the situation. We couldn't get under it. We couldn't get round it. We've had to go through it.

That lack of choice does not apply, however, to the spiritual journey that has run alongside or (perhaps a more appropriate image) underpinned the circumstances. Adrian and I have often been in a position where we could *choose* whether or not to accept God's will within the situation. At every turn of the road there has been another gate that we have had to make a conscious decision to enter.

Of course we could have chosen to say, 'Enough is enough'—not to what was happening to us but to the extent to which we allowed God to be a part of it. Rather than calling out as children to our Father for help, we could have decided to turn away from God and rely on our own finite resources. That has always been the human prerogative. And we have always had the chance to retrace our steps and start again, or ask to be renewed and refreshed and continue. It is the unique nature of our spiritual walk.

All this throws up an interesting question. Can you prepare for journeying with Christ or is it simply a matter of relying on the Holy Spirit to give you strength and inspiration day by day?

A few years ago I was talking to a member of one of our best-known Christian dance companies. She was telling me about one of the dilemmas they encounter when leading workshops around the country—the mindset that rejects formal training in favour of 'spiritual leading', that asks, 'How can the Holy Spirit truly lead you in worshipful dance if you are constrained by technical proficiency?'

Of course, that's pretty silly. The two are not mutually exclusive! I am very glad that most worship bands rely on their members having some honed musical skills and, all being well, the same applies to other art froms when put on public view. Equally valid, though, is the fact that, without divine inspiration and the input of the Holy Spirit, even the most elevated creative gifts are potentially sterile.

I think the same principle applies to the way we apply our faith to our lives, however dramatic the twists and turns. Every day we need to seek our Father's help and our Comforter's guidance but we also need to be resourced as much as possible. There are many ways in which we can prepare to follow our Lord and, in fact, Jesus told us to do just that.

Over the next week, we are going to take time to examine a few of those ways.

❖

Dear Father, many of us feel confused when we try to contemplate our journey so far. Sometimes it has been difficult to find you and stay close to you. Help us this week to think about what we can do to be ready for the next stage in our walk with you. For those of us starting out for the first time, show us how to prepare ourselves properly for the exciting journey ahead.

COUNTING THE COST

'You cannot come with me unless you love me more than you love your own life. You cannot be my disciple unless you carry your own cross and come with me. Suppose one of you wants to build a tower. What is the first thing you will do? Won't you sit down and figure out how much it will cost and if you have enough money to pay for it? Otherwise, you will start building the tower, but not be able to finish.'
LUKE 14:26–29

Counting the cost has strange connotations in today's society, where 'How would you like to pay?' is a question invariably asked whenever a purchase is made. Quite apart from choosing between store cards, debit and credit cards and old-fashioned cash, there are all the deferred options of the 'buy now, pay later' schemes.

Oh, we've been there! I can remember, all too well, Adrian and myself leaning back ecstatically in a luxurious plump sofa and a smiling sales assistant gently informing us that all this could be ours today—we didn't have to think about beginning to pay for it for a whole year. There wasn't a lot of 'Get thee behind me, Satan' in our response. We nearly joined the 'just sign here and worry about how the heck you're going to afford the repayments later' brigade. After all, 'anything can happen in a year', you tell yourself, dwelling on images of unknown millionaire relatives from far-off climes conveniently popping off. And anyway, we all know from the television that if you do get in a ghastly mess there are consolidation loan companies with benign smiley faces who are apparently happy to sort out everything for you at an affordable rate. The fact that the 'affordable rate' refers to interest that will effectively imprison you for life is not mentioned by the grateful recipients in the adverts.

Then there is the small print. Have you, like me, become an expert at counting the hidden costs in most 'amazing offers'? Postage and packing only £4.99 on an item that will weigh a few grammes at most and will fit into a padded envelope. And what about 'shipping costs + VAT not included'? Small wonder we have all become weary of being conned, and it is no surprise that we may look somewhat warily at the cost of following Jesus.

Let's get our minds clear on this: I am not talking about salvation. There is no small print attached to that free gift. All we have to do is receive it in full. No, I am talking about following Jesus, being a disciple, joining his army against the evil one, getting stuck in—in other words, 'walking the Way'. And that is where Jesus is determined that we should look carefully at what it might involve before leaping in.

'The thing is,' said a young German friend who has believed in Jesus for many years but does not feel she has left base camp yet, 'I don't know what I am signing up for. Suppose he wants to send me to China!'

I wasn't sure whether she meant that she baulked at the idea of the air fare or had some suspicions about how her heavenly Father might set about making her life as miserable as possible. There was no doubt that her worries were putting her off setting out along the Way at the moment. Maybe it was just as well. Too many of us have been enticed into a sort of 'buy now, probably won't ever have to pay later' type of Christian living that was never part of Jesus' advertising scheme. When he was here on earth, he was pretty tough about this, and there is no reason to suppose that he has changed since. For some, like Peter and James and John, following Jesus involved leaving the security of fishing businesses and probably causing considerable hardship to their families as a consequence. For Matthew, it meant leaving a lucrative job with all the perks that went with being in Roman pay. For the Samaritan woman at the well (John 4) and for Mary Magdalene, it involved a new way of life.

Two things seem significant to me about all this. One is that the cost varies a great deal from person to person. The other is that although Jesus' words in Luke 14 seem to insist that we are capable of giving up total rights to our selves *before* setting out, in fact many of his followers, notably Peter, had a lot of growing up to do along the way. We may not actually be asked, 'How would you like to pay?' as God has already decided the best scheme for us. In other words, we don't all have to sell everything we have, change our jobs or give up using our talents, but we need to do what we are personally asked to do by God. We may be asked to live by faith (without a steady source of income). Equally, we may not be asked to do this. We may be asked to give up some part of our lifestyle that has seemed fulfilling. Then again, we may not.

I've met several musicians and artists who gave up doing what they did best as soon as they became Christians, sure that God would not want them to continue with what they enjoyed and were good at doing. Thankfully, most of them have realized that they got this a bit wrong. In fact, most of us aren't asked to do anything very cataclysmic. The cost may well be in the form of no more than a 'few pence' a day, every day. Acknowledging someone in the street when you would prefer to pretend you haven't seen them. Being there for folk when you'd rather not bother. Giving time that could be 'me' time, putting what you want second. Over the years, giving in this way will add up to quite a lot but, instead of being a life sentence of debt, it will become a lifeline.

❖

Dear Father, we are all rich. You have given us so much. For some of us, it is money; for some of us, time; for some of us, talents. Help us to look a bit more honestly at our piggy banks and make some grown-up decisions about how much we are willing to give away. Help us to trust that, whatever you ask of us, it will never be more than we can bear. Help us to value what we are gaining in your service as a pearl beyond price, so that we give freely what we have to you today.

PACKING

The Lord says: My thoughts and my ways are not like yours. Just as the heavens are higher than the earth, my thoughts and my ways are higher than yours.
ISAIAH 55:8–9

It's a serious business, packing—deciding what to take and what not to take. I have an image imprinted in my mind, from a previous summer, of fifty 16-year-old girls arriving at their school gate ready for one week's watersports holiday in the south of France. Every one of them dragged a vast, bulging case or bag, some even carrying additional huge vanity bags for their make-up.

Clearly, other parents had had no more success than me in persuading their daughters that all they would need was swimwear, high factor suntan lotion, underwear, a few lightweight clothes and something warm for the evenings. Hairdryers, straighteners, several tons of make-up, shampoos and conditioners, and enough tops, jeans, shorts, high-heeled sandals and skirts for about a year, filled those perilously bulging bags. Other parents had probably also battled to persuade their young people that insect repellent was not as expendable as hair mousse.

Needless to say, the girls arrived home bronzed, beautiful and a bit rough round the edges, having enjoyed a fantastic make-up-free week and having used hardly any of the stuff that had seemed so 'absolutely must have' a week previously.

Then there is the packing-to-fly syndrome, where you pack

everything you know is going to be vital to your existence, weigh your case, scream, discard everything, look at it, put almost all of it back bit by bit and secretly decide to pay the excess!

We need to be properly kitted out, but just as I knew what my daughter would need for her holiday rather better than she did, so our Father God knows what we need and his list of necessities is not likely to be the same as ours.

What do we think we cannot do without in order to follow Jesus?

One of my favourite poems written by my husband is called, 'It Is Finished'. Based on some of the words uttered by Jesus from the cross, it looks at the challenges we face as Christians to continue his work.

> *It is finished.*
> *I don't think so.*
> *Not yet...*

> *Not until I freely place my stock of cherished certainties*
> *Like sad surrendered weapons at your injured feet...*

I honestly think that our firmly held 'certainties' take up the largest amount of space in our spiritual luggage and are considered by us as indispensable. Most of us learn at a pretty young age that having an opinion enables us to escape unscathed from many situations. 'Well, what I've always thought is...' It means we don't have to risk going through a potential minefield that might make us feel uncertain and uneasy. Our minds are already made up. No further discussion is necessary.

When I first went to university, 'Evolution versus Creation' was the big issue (that shows how old I am!). A while ago, it was the role of women in the church. Now it's homosexuality. Tomorrow— who knows?

I am aware that tolerance taken to its limits can be dangerous. It can be a counterfeit of true love, which sometimes has to be tough to be kind. It can store up problems for the future of humanity. Its liberality can suggest that there is no such thing as absolute truth. I think, however, that we should allow ourselves the possibility that there is more to most debates than we may have thought so far. There is possibly a 'third way' of thinking, which will require courage and vision and could involve us stepping 'outside the frame' in order to see clearly the whole picture.

The newest debate threatening our stability is about the nature of church. The Church of Scotland has launched an initiative called *Church without Walls*, which is exploring what church in the 21st century needs to be if it is to meet the needs of society flexibly, yet without compromise. Will progress forward involve accepting that church as we know it might have to decline in order to be restored, or even die in order to be resurrected? Do we have to acknowledge that the walls of organized religion are crumbling?

Of course, opening our stash of certainties to the scrutiny of our Father in heaven may mean that we are asked to do some drastic repacking but, if so, we are in good company. Think of the disciples. Poor Peter and co. No two days with Jesus were the same, although I do hope there were a few ordinary days when they all got up, did ordinary things, had ordinary meals, talked ordinary talk and had an early night. Imagine the shocks and surprises, the twists and turns of following a leader who was constantly open to doing what he heard his Father in heaven telling him to do.

'We don't like Samaritans. Never have. Bad lot, if you ask me. Ah, Jesus is talking to one of them—and a woman, too... Now he's converting a whole village of them. Oh, and the point of the story of the good Samaritan is... Ah, I see...'

'Now come on, be reasonable women, Jesus won't want to be pestered by your children. He's exhausted and he... does want to see and talk to your children...'

'Oh, the Sabbath is made for man, not... But I thought—oh...'
'We touch lepers?!'
'We party with tax collectors?!!'
'The Pharisees might not be right?!!!'

The truth is, they didn't shine very often, did they? But the crucial point has to be that however much they failed, when challenged they didn't turn away. After all, as Peter said, 'To whom shall we go? You have the words of eternal life' (John 6:68, NIV).

They kept following right behind, the way ahead so increasingly narrow that they couldn't see what they would encounter next, their stock of cherished-certainty weapons proving useless, dwindling fast, their bags ever lighter, their dependence ever greater.

❖

Dear Father, please help me to look at whatever I have in my luggage that you would like me to discard. Show me which firmly held opinions you would like jettisoned. Please help me to be brave enough to lay them at your feet and leave them there, trusting in you and you alone for my safety and my future.

TRAVEL LIGHT AND SEE WHERE YOU'RE GOING

Jesus sent out the twelve apostles with these instructions: '… Don't take along any gold, silver, or copper coins. And don't carry a travelling bag or an extra shirt or sandals or a walking stick.'

MATTHEW 10:5, 10–11

We have looked at some things we need to jettison before setting off. So what *do* we need to pack for our journey? Very little, according to Jesus, but why?

Why did Jesus give such instructions to those who were setting out to preach the gospel, heal the sick and generally preach the good news? He made it very clear that he wanted his followers to be vulnerable—'like lambs into a pack of wolves' (Matthew 10:16) —but doesn't it seem rather mean, and maybe rather shortsighted, to send them out so frugally equipped?

Maybe it was so that they would be seen as a contrast to the rich rabbis who customarily lorded it over ordinary folk. Maybe it was to encourage generosity among their hosts. And maybe, also, it was so that they could focus on their task without being distracted by their possessions or weighed down by the responsibilty of preserving them intact.

I have travelled round the world more than once with four children. I can honestly say that, leaving aside the odd moment when I could have cheerfully murdered them all, wherever we went they themselves were the least of my worries. It was their cricket bats and hats and footballs and cameras and passports and sunglasses and postcards and books and games and soft toys and so on that caused the problems. We once had to pay for Gregory, a small battered bear belonging to our daughter, to travel from Sydney, Australia, to Hailsham, East Sussex, after he had been left behind on our travels. Other Plass belongings are probably still dismally trying to find their way home from Down Under. Since those journeys, we have never felt deprived when circumstances dictate that we pack only essentials. In fact, travelling light has become a luxury.

Mind you, we should have learnt that lesson many years ago.

When Adrian and I got married, we were poor. I don't mean the sort of 'poor' where you don't have any ready cash but you do have a mortgage, a pension scheme and a savings account. Neither, I should add, do I mean Third World poor, where having enough rice in the bowl to prevent you from starving is the measure of riches. I mean not having enough money for a house, a honeymoon or even a hangover!

Being hard up didn't worry us overmuch but we did so want a honeymoon. We were working as residential social workers with maladjusted children at the time, and were seriously exhausted. We hit on a solution. Not for us a wedding present list consisting of household equipment. After all, we hadn't got a house. No, we would ask for really useful things—like a tent, sleeping bags, rucksacks and camping gas cookers.

The honeymoon was sorted—or so we thought. Unfortunately we forgot to remind people that we had no car and couldn't afford trains and buses. We also forgot to say that as we would be hitch-hiking we would be carrying our holiday home and its contents on our backs. It was an omission that hit us only when we happily waved goodbye to the assembled guests and set off for Cornwall. The tent we had been given was without doubt the heaviest tent ever invented, accompanied by a ludicrously huge, unruly bag of bulky poles. The sleeping bags were the sort that look innocent enough while encased in their slim plastic bags but, when released, uncurl into monsters of gigantic proportions and refuse ever to be tamed again. The rucksacks were the cheap, lumpy sort that mean you invariably perform a Hunchback of Notre Dame impression whenever you walk more than a few yards—that is, if you could get started in the first place.

Our morning ritual went something like this. First, standing with my back to Adrian, I would bend back as far as I could, while he strapped my rucksack on to my shoulders. Then with immense effort, and with him taking as much of the weight as he could I swung my whole body forward so that I was bending until I could almost touch my toes. Adrian would then adjust the straps and help me regain a semi-vertical position before we set off.

I could see nothing of the countryside, so bowed down was I by my small share of our belongings. I couldn't talk as I had to reserve every bit of puff for walking. All I could focus on was the back of my new husband's feet, and even they frequently disappeared from view completely, leaving me feeling abandoned and lonely as he strode ahead a couple of hundred yards, then dumped his load and returned to relieve me temporarily of my burden. To onlookers it must have seemed as if we were taking part in some obscure ritual or obstacle race. We eventually curtailed our plans of exploring the whole of the Lizard peninsular, and settled down for an idyllic week of not carrying anything anywhere.

When Jesus suggested that we should travel light, his intention was not that we should feel deprived and hard done by but that we should enjoy the experience of walking with him without the distraction of being weighed down by our creature comforts. He wants us to have enough breath to talk to him, to be able to see the beauty of the countryside, and to feel safe following our completely visible guide.

❖

Dear Father, help us to accept that you know best. Show us what we need to dump in order to make our load lighter, so that walking with you becomes the pleasure it was for those first followers of the Way.

RECOGNIZING HIS VOICE

Jesus said: '... The sheep know their shepherd's voice. He calls each of them by name and leads them out. When he has led out all his sheep, he walks in front of them, and they follow because they know his voice.'
JOHN 10:1, 3–4

You can be certain that in the last days there will be some very hard times. People will love only themselves and money. They will be proud, stuck-up, rude, and disobedient to their parents. They will also be ungrateful, godless, heartless, and hateful. Their words will be cruel, and they will have no self-control or pity. These people will hate everything that is good. They will be sneaky, reckless, and puffed up with pride. Instead of loving God, they will love pleasure. Even though they will make a show of being religious, their religion won't be real.
2 TIMOTHY 3:1–5

One area of training that we need to get our heads round in order to be ready for the adventure of following Christ is that of learning to distinguish our guide's voice.

My father's family come from Clitheroe in Lancashire. One of the treats involved in visiting this part of the world is to drive or walk through the stunning moorland pass, the Trough of Bowland. One year, our visit coincided with lambing time, and everywhere we went we were entertained by the entrancing sight of lambs playing together in their own unique way—no other young creatures gambol!

The questions of how their mothers could tell them apart, and whether the babies would ever manage to sort out which ewe was their source of dinner were answered over and over again in front of our eyes. First we would hear a mother's deep bass call and, looking out over the hillsides dotted with small lambs, it seemed impossible that her baby would identify its mother's voice. But eventually we would hear a tiny cry and see in the distance a small woolly shape extricate itself from its playmates to come tottering down the steep slopes for an ecstatic reunion with its anxious mother.

If it had been just one mother calling and one lamb responding, it would not have been so amazing, but the miracle lies in the fact that all the mothers and all the lambs seemed to be shouting at each other at the same time. It's a loud world out there in the Trough of Bowland in the spring! Clearly each mum and each lamb sounded distinctly different, but you had to be a sheep to interpret the difference.

When we become children of God, we begin to hear our Father's voice calling us, but because we have not always been in his family we have to learn to distinguish his voice from all the other voices of our megaphonic world. When we start to follow him seriously, it is a matter of life and death that we learn this skill as well as we can, but how?

Some time ago, my mother admitted that she was in need of a new hearing aid having reluctantly accepted that not everyone she met could possibly have conspired to whisper at the same time. After a lengthy consultation and fitting of her new digital device, we decided to have lunch in the shopping mall. We stayed in our seats for about four minutes, until my poor mother put her hands over her ears in despair. Her head felt as if it was going to burst. We were hardly in the middle of an ear-destroying pop concert, but I realized immediately what was going on. I didn't know until the audiologist told me that one of the brain's many tasks is to discern between the sound of important information and lesser background noises. We can cope with washing machines humming and heating systems gurgling quietly in the background while we talk undisturbed. My mother's brain, albeit presumably delighted at being given aural messages again after months of imposed silence, was freaking out under the barrage of sound which it had not had time to filter out.

We hear loud voices blasting from the media, and especially advertisements, insisting that they have important, even vital, information for us. We may hear equally strident voices from our church leaders. We need to ask for spiritual discernment to filter out what is harmless background noise, to discard what is insistent and harmful to our inner ear and to know with ever-increasing certainty the small but strong voice of God, which will keep us safe and give us the peace the world craves but has no idea how to find.

We will need to know which voices to reject on our journey. Most of us need to learn how to fine-tune our hearing so that we will recognize the voice of Satan and be able to tell him to go away even when his suggestions sound like sweet music to our human ear. We may be able to distinguish between the discordant voices of religious and political fanaticism and our master's voice, but what about more subtle, more melodious voices ?

It is by reading God's living word—the Bible—that we will learn to recognize his voice and increase our chances of staying safe from the evil one. For example, can a one-sided theology that tells us God's blessing lies only in the area of material wealth come from the mouth of the one who told us to be prepared to give up everything to follow him? Can a voice telling us that we will know we are on the Way only if we are happy and well be that of the good shepherd?

Whatever your views on the war in Iraq, I wonder if anyone else experienced the chill of fear I did when I heard that the USA, apparently a God-fearing nation, was planning to use 'shock and awe' tactics. The dictionary definition of 'awe' is 'reverential fear' and there is no doubt that in that first mighty assault on the city of Baghdad the plan was to exhibit a God-like show of strength, might, power and wealth. This fits uncomfortably with the message of Jesus when he is telling his followers that it is the humble who will inherit the earth! (Matthew 5:5).

Look at the extraordinary words of Mary who, filled to bursting with the Holy Spirit, poured out the song we now call the Magnificat (Luke 1:46–55):

> *God All-Powerful has done great things for me,*
> *and his name is holy.*
> *He always shows mercy*
> *to everyone who worships him.*
> *The Lord has used his powerful arm*
> *to scatter those who are proud.*
> *He drags strong rulers from their thrones*
> *and puts humble people in places of power.*

❖

Dearest Father, remind us today, we beg you, what your voice sounds like. Please help us to get better at identifying when it is you speaking, so that when the other voices come we will be able to reject them.

GET IN SHAPE

All of you are slow to understand. By now you should have been teachers but once again you need to be taught the simplest things about what God has said. You need milk instead of solid food. People who live on milk are like babies who don't really know what is right. Solid food is for mature people who have been trained to know right from wrong. We must try to become mature and start thinking about more than just the basic things we were taught about Christ... We shouldn't need to keep teaching about baptisms or about the laying on of hands or about people being raised from death and the future judgment. Let's grow up, if God is willing.

HEBREWS 5:11—6:3

On the face of it, this is a bit confusing, isn't it? The issues that the author of Hebrews describes as 'basics' seem to constitute quite a hearty diet. For example, baptism has fuelled many an energetic argument among disciples through the ages, while people being raised from the dead is hardly the everyday pattern of infant Christians. If this is milk, what on earth is meat?

Well, perhaps typically, the ultimate solid food designed to give us energy for a long and healthy life is not going to be found in theological tomes but in the simple but hard challenges of obedience. This is what Jesus spoke of when he was sitting by Jacob's well in Samaria after talking to the woman with five ex-husbands. When the disciples begged him to eat something, Jesus told them he had food that they didn't know about, and when they jumped to the conclusion that someone else had brought him lunch, he set them straight with the words, 'My food is to do what God wants' (John 4:31–34).

So there we have it. This, better than any other diet, could keep us in tip-top condition. Mind you, we may not look like a good advertisement for it on the outside. Our bodies might still end up looking a bit worn and neglected. It is the 'internal body', the bit that lives for eternity, that will be glowing with health.

Like most effective diets, this one is essentially simple. It is also, for us with all our human cravings, nearly impossible for us to stick to. So while we hold it in our minds as the ideal to aim at, let us look realistically at what we might try in order to increase our fitness.

Any dietician will tell us that the first step is to be honest about what we are eating. We need to put under the spotlight whether or not we are eating a balanced diet, and look at the extent to which we are indulging the child in us, who craves treats, sweeties and comfort foods. Spiritual 'comfort foods' might contain too high a content of Bible readings that dwell solely on happy happenings and angel visitations, and demand nothing of us. Or we might be sidetracked into the 'myths and endless genealogies' that Paul mentions in 1 Timothy 1:4 (NIV), which could certainly give us indigestion. Eating healthily will not usually mean drastically cutting out all such things, so those of us who feel the urge to indulge in a helping of 'future judgment' will probably be allowed a small portion occasionally. Balance is the key, and for some of us that might mean radical reform. No more binging on 'end times'. No more anorexic starving on mysticism.

It might involve trying new foods which have, until now, seemed unpalatable. That was Peter's experience when he was given a dream in which he was shown that he was to eat food that was forbidden by Jewish law (Acts 10:9–16). His acceptance of what the 'head dietician' wanted for him opened the way for people to eat of the bread of life who had so far not been allowed even a taste: Peter realized that the gospel was for Gentiles as well as Jews.

Or maybe we will be asked to try something more adventurous. The 'I'm a pie-and-peas sort of bloke' may even enjoy a chicken fajita if he were prepared to give it a go. The same old stuff day in, day out can be very boring and unimaginative and can also be a real turn-off for those you provide for.

It may involve us using our common sense to avoid diets that are simply unbalanced. It's tempting to seize upon a particular portion of scripture as being the answer to our dietary needs, to the exclusion of all else. This way of eating is bad for us because it softens our brains. Many of those who have gorged on Mark 16:18 have the snake bites to prove this. Worse still, such a diet can lead to a hardening of the heart and be a contributory factor in evils as appalling as apartheid. When we discover what God wants for us, we can be so sure it must be right for everyone else that we shove it down their throats until they are sick. Some of us have convinced ourselves, just like my children's friends coming for tea when they were small, that we are allergic to whatever we don't like. Some of us are faddy eaters, refusing with a shudder to touch anything we think might interfere with our delicate digestive systems. A bowl of inner-city living has far too much fibre for most of our tastes!

Using our common sense might keep us safe from cranky diets that promise miracle cures and quick fixes. We all clamour for immediate effects, and if such a diet is endorsed by the rich and famous, all the better. In our celebrity-soaked society, we desperately want to be special too, to be one of the 'beautiful people'. We will go to enormous lengths to get our hands on the relevant information. Then we sing its praises until we have to face the fact that it isn't working as fast as we thought it should, whereupon we are in danger of being disillusioned not only with that particular diet but with any attempt to be more food-conscious.

A while ago, there was said to be an extraordinary aromatic brew bubbling away in the Canadian city of Toronto. There was little doubt that it was authentically heavenly food with life-enhancing properties, and it caused great excitement, the wonderful aroma spreading throughout the world. We lifted our noses like Bisto kids and longed for a taste. Our mouths watered, our spiritual taste buds tingled and many of us became convinced that this food was vital for our continuing health. I personally know several people who were prepared to spend a great deal of money to travel to the city in order to be sure of receiving their share, and I know of one church so greedy for a spoonful of this elixir that they stamped their feet and demanded it from their elders as vociferously as children tugging at their mother's arm in the supermarket queue because they have seen the sweet stand. Some people pretended they had some, even when they knew they hadn't. Others lost confidence because they hadn't been given any and felt like giving up. It was all a bit ridiculous really.

How silly we are! We will do almost anything to avoid the simple fact that getting into shape means aiming to eat sensibly. It involves hard work, initiative and discipline and, all being well, will become a way of life.

What is a balanced faith diet? What will sustain us on our journey with God? The staple food is, of course, the bread of life, Jesus himself (John 6:48). The ingredients of good bread are simple but wholesome. Without huge chunks of it, through prayer and feeding on his word, we will become undernourished. There is also living water (John 4:10) which cleanses our systems and quenches our thirst in a way no other liquid can. We need to come to Jesus and drink—through worship, through experiencing God's creation, through those we love. There is fibre in the day-to-day challenges God sets us, and protein in the richness of community. We will find essential salts of human kindness, and sweetness in our forgiveness of others. And of course there are glucose and vitamin-packed treats—God's forgiveness, his love, his belief in us, his acceptance of us—all these are concentrated into a spiritual version of Kendal mint cake for us walkers to snack on whenever we need a shot of energy.

There's one more thing: most diets suggest eating little but often and giving yourself time to digest what you have consumed before reaching out for more food. The manna God gave to the people of Israel only lasted for a day, thus keeping them dependent and safe (Exodus 16:19–20). It cannot be for nothing that Jesus urged us to ask God to 'Give us each day our *daily* bread' (Luke 11:3, NRSV).

❖

Take time today to look at what is sustaining you. Do you deliberately stick to the comforting passages in the Bible? Or refuse to read them at all? Are you so convinced that your way of eating spiritual food is good enough that you are not prepared to change at all? How much is the fitness of your inner self a priority? Try asking the real expert, who knows your individual requirements, to get involved in creating a diet just for you. If you need detoxing, why not give it a try?

FUEL FOR THE JOURNEY

I pray that his Spirit will make you become strong followers and that Christ will live in your hearts because of your faith. Stand firm and be deeply rooted in his love. I pray that you and all God's people will understand what is called wide or long or high or deep. I want you to know all about Christ's love, although it is too wonderful to be measured. Then your lives will be filled with all that God is. I pray that Christ Jesus and the church will for ever bring praise to God. His power at work in us can do far more than we dare ask or imagine.

EPHESIANS 3:16–21

Many years ago, Adrian recorded for posterity a journey that has become a family joke against yours truly. After weeks of planning and shopping and making lists, I spent several hours packing for a week's holiday at a Christian camp where Adrian was to be one of the speakers. I then spent almost as long loading our three boys and the camping gear into our not-big-enough car. At last we were ready and cheerfully set off, only to come to a complete halt half a mile down the road.

Petrol had not been on my list, you see. Toilet rolls and sleeping bags and kites and buckets and spades and dustbin bags and Bibles and food and bedtime books... yes. Fuel... no.

Why do things so often go wrong because of some small but vital lack of forethought? Like having to give up a hike because of a blister and no plasters. The grand sweep of things—the dream, the vision—reduced to nothing because of a trifling detail.

Adrian and I, at the time of writing, are learning a great deal about the importance of detail and the necessity for plenty of the right kind of fuel. At the moment we have the privilege of looking after my mother in our home. She is very, very poorly. The sweeping grand gesture is redundant now. Plans for the future have no relevance. Making sure that she has a straw to drink her water from a cup light enough for her to hold is important. So is using sufficient talcum powder on the bedpan; brushing her hair; cleaning her teeth; supporting her aching head; preparing delicate tiny meals and throwing them away untouched… not crying.

Ours has become a small world, life reduced to minutiae for the time we have her. Love for her is our fuel. It doesn't transfigure the unpleasant jobs, but there is a real joy in preserving her self-respect and dignity which makes even the most ghastly things possible. It enables us to smile and joke with her during her little windows of relaxation. It lends us courage to speak the truth to her without fudging it. It determines that we will be with her to the end, whatever the cost. It really has become service with a smile.

Our call to discipleship is a call to service—service which will feel burdensome, dry and often downright unpleasant if it is not motivated by love. Love and respect are not optional extras on our walk with God, any more than the petrol in my car was on that summer holiday so many years ago. You can try to manage without them till the cows come home, but you will make no more progress than we could in our petrol-less car. Indeed, we would have been sitting in our country lane until the cows had come home if we hadn't refuelled!

Adrian and I are the lucky ones. It is not hard to love and respect my mother, but I have to admit that we had no idea whether or not we would be capable of caring for her adequately before we took the step of inviting her to come to live with us, after the discovery of inoperable cancer. We wanted to do it with all our hearts but dreaded failing, knowing how costly and consuming of time and emotion love 'in detail' is. But just as our respect and love for her increases day by day as she lives out her life in our ex-dining room, so I believe our love and respect for God will grow and flourish, once we make the decision to risk going for what we know is right. Only when we have taken that risk will we have a chance of discovering the extraordinary depths of his love.

What if you are feeling that God has forfeited such love and respect—perhaps by heaping on you the very type of undeserved tragedy I am describing here? You may want to continue to move forward but your tank is almost dry. Well, for starters, accept that you are coming to a halt. Stop pretending that everything is OK between you and God if it isn't. Stop kidding yourself that you love him if you don't. Look on today as a day when you take time to find out just how much fuel you have in your tank. Of course you can't manufacture or buy the kind of fuel you need to move forward spiritually. There is only one source of the sort of love that will keep you going to the end. If you are running low, you must ask to be topped up—and keep asking. He has promised that if you ask you will receive (Matthew 7:7). This is one promise I think we need to claim.

Many years ago, I watched my husband collapse defeated, as a result of a crisis illness that almost destroyed his belief in the love of God. It was in his poetry that I learnt most about his inner struggles and in his poetry that I saw the first signs of his tentative belief that it just might be possible to pick himself up and move forward again. One of these snippet poems was called 'I watch':

> I watch
> Frightened
> Helpless
> But secretly willing
> As my foot rises, moving forward with my weight,
> And I realize
> That at last
> I am going to walk.

I truly believe we can trust that if we take the first few steps towards doing what we know God is calling us to do, however frightened we are by the unknown, he will honour our 'secret willingness'. As, minute by minute, hour by hour, day by day, we slowly learn to concentrate on the details of the task he has given us, we will begin to experience his love again, and feel encouraged and enabled to move forward.

❖

Dear Father, so many of us are afraid that if we look into our fuel tank we will find it is very low. We have angers and hurts and doubts that we know need filtering out but we have not the expertise or energy to do anything about it. Yet deep down we still want to follow you. Help us to examine the details of our loves and our lives and our relationship with you. And, Father, help us to trust that you love us enough not to fudge the truth.

STAYING SAFE

(The guidelines of Jesus)

When you fall through the holes in your life,
Don't think it surprising or odd,
Be glad that it's planned you will finally land,
On the solid forgiveness of God.

© ADRIAN PLASS

FOLLOW *THE* LEADER

'Stay away from those Pharisees! They are like blind people leading other blind people, and all of them will fall into a ditch.'
MATTHEW 15:14

Look after yourselves and everyone the Holy Spirit has placed in your care. Be like shepherds to God's church. It is the flock that he bought with the blood of his own Son. I know that after I am gone, others will come like fierce wolves to attack you. Some of your own people will tell lies to win over the Lord's followers. Be on your guard! Remember how day and night for three years I warned you with tears in my eyes. I now place you in God's care.
ACTS 20:28–32

You were doing so well until someone made you turn from the truth. And that person was certainly not sent by the one who chose you. A little yeast can change a whole batch of dough, but you belong to the Lord.
GALATIANS 5:7–10

Jesus was in a very serious mood when he talked to his friends about the dangers that they would confront on their journey forward without him to lead and protect them.

These dangers were reiterated again and again by Paul to his fragile newly formed churches. On one occasion, when he decided he would not have time to visit his church in Ephesus, he actually called all the leaders together for an emergency meeting on the island of Miletus to remind them how vigilant they needed to be (Acts 20:17). Some of his words to them are quoted in the Bible passage above. There is just so much both within and outside us to entice us off the path that God has chosen for us to walk.

In our first Bible passage, Jesus is asking us to use our common sense. There is a lot of liberating talk about empowerment in our churches at present, and, where people have been encouraged to discover their genuine gifting, there is exciting evidence of growth in creativity and strength. However, we would probably feel justified in dissuading someone with no musical training whatsoever from playing for our Sunday worship. We would apply same criteria to a walk up a mountain, preferably choosing a Sherpa to lead us. Or, to use Jesus' illustration, we would not choose someone who is blind to lead us along a narrow path, thus hugely increasing our chances of falling into ditches.

It's common sense, yet many of us have tried, sometimes desperately, to subdue the stirrings of this God-given attribute when listening to someone standing up at the front in church. It feels embarrassingly earthbound to be yearning to point out the obvious flaws in someone's apparently Spirit-led vision—especially when, like the little boy observing the emperor's 'new clothes', we seem to be the only one who can see that something is strangely amiss. Maybe we should follow our earthly instincts more often. Maybe we would do well to question, as Paul encouraged his followers to do, whether this particular leader has been sent by 'the one who chose us'.

Paul's letter to the church in Galatia was dealing with a very serious matter. The suggestion that circumcision was imperative for those deciding to become Christians was threatening to place all new Gentile converts under Jewish law, and was totally at variance with the good news of salvation. You can hear the anguish and anxiety in Paul's message, as well as the affection he clearly had for the people in this church. 'You were doing so well until someone made you turn from the truth.'

I have a feeling that a lot of the messes we find ourselves in could have been avoided if we had only used our brains a bit more!

Paul's emphasis in Acts and Galatians was on the dangers from outside. The lies and deceptions and false impressions put about by the 'wolves' can destroy us. One of these false impressions is the image of the narrow way as a pharisaical route march on which we are likely to die of thirst because of all the things we would not be allowed to consume. I don't think Jesus would have walked the 'thou shalt not' road for long. He would have been off at every turning to meet someone else made sad by sin, and encouraging them to join him.

Then there are those denominational 'wolves' who are so arrogant that they see the narrow way as a path they and they alone are on. A while ago, a close friend of ours was telling us about the stern disapproval that was expressed when he, a young committed Christian of strict Brethren upbringing, wanted to marry a devout Baptist. Mind you, the 'I'm right' mindset can affect those who consider themselves above denominational trivialities. i once sat in a meeting and listened to an apparently reasoned argument by a well-known preacher as to why *all* denominations—yes, *all*—were no longer part of the body of Christ inhabited by the living Holy Spirit and were merely dead limbs that should be discarded to the abbatoir where they belonged. As I said, a lot of the messes we find ourselves in could be avoided if we only used our brains more.

This week we are going to take some time to read the safety rules that Jesus, Paul and Peter laid down to keep us on the straight and narrow, both by using our common sense and by avoiding the fierce wolves.

❖

Dear Father, you tried so hard to set before us rules that would keep us safe from the evil one. Forgive us for the times when we have been downright silly, when we have not listened, and when we have been tempted to trot off behind blind leaders. Help us to look again with open eyes at some of the advice you gave us.

YOUR JOURNEY
AND YOURS ALONE

Be alert and think straight. Put all your hope in how kind God will be to you when Jesus Christ appears. Behave like obedient children. Don't let your lives be controlled by your desires, as they used to be.

1 PETER 1:13–14

We must stop acting like children. We must not let deceitful people trick us by their false teachings, which are like winds that toss us around from place to place. Love should always make us tell the truth. Then we will grow in every way and be more like Christ, the head of the body. Christ holds it together and makes all its parts work perfectly, as it grows and becomes strong because of love.

EPHESIANS 4:14–16

Don't compare yourself with others. We each must carry our own load.

GALATIANS 6:4–5

Here Peter and Paul both emphasize the unique truth of the Christian way. You need to be sensible and adult but, paradoxically, that means being childlike in obedience, open to discipline and care from others, and open to the fact that you have little idea where you are going and what you are doing.

I was talking to a newly qualified doctor recently. She had qualified with distinction in several subjects and, full of confidence, arrived on the hospital ward to discover that she knew nothing! Of course, in time, her knowledge began to return to inform her decisions, but for a while, aware that what she said and did could be a matter not of an exam mark but of real life or real death, she felt unsure and frightened.

When we agree to follow Jesus seriously, we can and should prepare as much as possible, but if we mean business God may well place us in situations that make us feel inadequate and useless. The answer that sounds so good in a Bible study sounds hollow and useless when challenged by real live unbelievers. The faith that sustained us so easily on the 'dry land' of a Sunday morning can seem flimsy and insubstantial when we are all at sea, out of our depth, and the waves are rocking our makeshift boat.

Growing up means that we have to take responsibility for our sins. One of the compliments that Jesus paid women, who were considered at the time to be no more mature than children, was that he *expected* them to be capable of discipling themselves in the area of sin. If Jesus said to any one of them, as he did to the woman caught in the act of adultery, 'Go and sin no more', he expected that they would at least try to carry out his command. He believed that they were capable of making courageous, difficult decision to being about changes in the way they lived their lives.

Those of us who have had a child or looked after one will remember at least one occasion when the child took something they shouldn't have touched and then concealed it behind their back when they realized they'd been found out. At times like this, you say, 'What have you got behind your back?' and the child, eyes wide with innocence, declares against all the evidence, 'Nothing!'

Children are only sorry and guilty when they are caught and their misdemeanours are pointed out. If loved and disciplined, those children will grow up to be really sorry for causing sadness and worry to those who love and care about them, and this will begin to inform their behaviour. It is unimaginative immaturity that explains why criminals can act so selfishly.

Growing up means that we have to take responsibility for our own behaviour too. I have had four teenagers. I know all about what 'everybody else' apparently does or doesn't do as regards homework and schoolwork and bed times and playing computer games. Why aim higher than your peers?

This attitude doesn't automatically go away when we get older. We all tend to sink to the level of the lowest common denominator. How easy it is to feel comfortable about your efforts if you compare them only to those in your immediate circle! If we gauge holiness only by looking at folk in our particular church or community, we can be lulled into thinking that we are living much as God intended. After all, if old so-and-so thinks it's all right... then it must be all right for me too. You must know the sort of thing!

Growing up in God will also mean allowing the child in us to play again—to speak out, to say what we see, to be unafraid to take risks and unafraid to say what we think and to display affection and hurt. But dare we?

Look at what else Peter says: 'Put all your hope in how *kind* God will be to you when Jesus appears.' I think we can do that.

❖

Dear Father, help us to look at where we are being childish in not taking responsibility for our walk with you. Show us where we are being immature in our discipleship. Open our eyes to see the truth and speak out what we see to others.

KEEPING OUR LOVED ONES ON THE PATH WITH US

What if I could speak all languages of humans and of angels? If I did not love others, I would be nothing more than a noisy gong or a clanging cymbal... And what if I had faith that moved mountains? I would be as nothing, unless I loved others. What if I gave away all that I owned and let myself be burnt alive? I would gain nothing, unless I loved others.

1 CORINTHIANS 13:1–3

My friends, you are spiritual. So if someone is trapped in sin, you should gently lead that person back to the right path. But watch out, and don't be tempted yourself.

GALATIANS 6:1

If we keep on loving others, we will stay united in our hearts with God, and he will stay united with us. If we truly love others and live as Christ did in this world, we won't be worried about the day of judgment. A real love for others will chase those worries away. The thought of being punished is what makes us afraid. It shows that we have not really learnt to love.

1 JOHN 4:16–18

Somehow we can't help feeling that our spiritual life would be a lot less complicated or that we would stand far more chance of staying on the path if it wasn't for those with whom we live in close proximity. The well-known words from 1 Corinthians 13 remind us that, as usual, God isn't interested in grandiose promises or empty sacrifices. By loving responsibly those whom we have been given to care for, we not only keep them safe but ourselves as well.

I have met many young mothers who feel confused by the difficulty they are experiencing in what they see as a 'real' walk with Christ, hampered as they are by those well-known prayer wreckers, toddlers. Then there are those caring for elderly relatives, whose age has created a demand that wears their carers down and can make them feel resentful.

Recently I was talking to a young single woman who had joined a thriving Christian community. She had imagined it would make her Christian life far more fulfilling. After a few weeks of washing up, cleaning and living closely with a large group of fellow believers, she began to doubt whether God actually existed at all!

And then there is marriage. I doubt if it's possible to sort out, before marriage, which of your failings will create the big difficulties. Most people talk about how coming home from the honeymoon is the big eye-opener. I reckon I got my first inkling earlier than that. The first few days of our honeymoon, once we had put down our rucksacks, were as idyllic as we could have wished. The sun shone on our isolated blue and orange tent as we drank a lot of cheap wine, ate a lot of good food and blissfully explored the Padstow area. Then we hitched down to Zennor, which had looked very exciting and romantic in our delightfully biased John Betjeman's *Guide to Cornwall*. Betjeman must have been to a different Zennor! We ended up in a mushy field of nettles next to a bull, with no access to the beach, in gale force winds and relentless rain.

On the second morning, the rain pounded on to the hood of my anorak as I crouched over our tiny stove. I was cooking bacon and eggs. My fringe, soaked into rat's tails, dangled miserably into my eyes and shot drops of water rhythmically into the hot bacon fat. The hot bacon fat bounced rhythmically and painfully back into my face. The knees of my trendy new 'holiday' jeans were reduced to two blocks of soggy smelly mud. I was, to put it mildly utterly fed up.

'This is the nearest thing to heaven I can imagine.'

Turning and peering through the wet rags of my fringe, I stared at my newlywed nearest and dearest lying comfortably in his sleeping bag, a No 6 alight in one hand and a book open in the other. He beamed at me. That beam lived dangerously. For the first time I wondered if it was going to be much fun living for the rest of my life with someone who could be so amazingly oblivious to practical issues. It didn't seem so romantically bohemian on that wet, cold, clifftop morning, and there have been numerous times since when I'd gladly have swapped him, albeit temporarily, for one of the 'put up those shelves in a jiffy' sort. Equally, there have been many times when I'm sure he'd have given me away.

Many of the things we thought we had in common before marrying have stood the test of time, although when we sat down a while ago to make a list, we weren't over-impressed by other similarities that had crept in over the years. For instance, rather high up on our list came 'a willingness to collude in time wasting'. We've realized how often we take it in turns to rationalize this tendency. We're both awfully good at finding excellent reasons why we should postpone the boring task in hand and do something else.

'A love of cream teas' didn't seem very impressive, either. Other similarities included a love of acting and performing, a sympathy for or empathy with small people and 'losers', and a sense of inadequacy when side-by-side with super-efficient or ultra-smart types. We both thrive on encouragement and collapse under severe criticism. We both love *Diary of a Nobody*, *Three Men in a Boat*, *Just William* and *The Wind in the Willows*. Neither of us understands opera. We both loathe meanness, petty-mindedness and bullying. We both admire the 'extra-milers' we have met, more than we admire anyone else. We would both describe ourselves as relative thinkers, preferring to live in the mystery than trying to tie up every spiritual loose end.

Then there are the differences: Adrian hates gardening; I love it. Adrian loves cricket; I think it's boring. Adrian adores rain; I think it's wet. Adrian cares passionately about whether or not Rutland is a separate county. I…?!

Similarities and differences can both be invigorating. They can prevent the relationship from just slumping. They can also be destructive and exhausting, especially when collusion against the alleged unfairness of God and others creeps in. Where two or three are gathered together, an awful lot of nonsense can be agreed on!

Perhaps the greatest dangers of a close relationship, speaking from my own experience, is that we can so easily hold each other back or shove each other forward without realizing that what we want is approval. We so want those we love to be respected, liked and accepted by those in authority that we are in danger of preventing God from getting a word in edgeways. Our job is to care for the child within the person we love, to nurture their changing and maturing and to respect their individual calling, even if it means that sometimes we are asked to let one of us go it alone on an unknown path.

❖

Dear Father, help us to give you the responsibility for those we love. Give us discernment so that we cannot be tempted to be less than you want us to be, and love so that we can set them free to have their own adventure in you.

TRAVEL TOGETHER

Jesus... looked up towards heaven and prayed:

'... You have given me some followers from this world, and I have shown them what you are like. They were yours, but you gave them to me, and they have obeyed you... I told my followers what you told me, and they accepted it... I am praying for them, but not for those who belong to this world. My followers belong to you, and I am praying for them... Holy Father, I am no longer in the world. I am coming to you, but my followers are still in the world. So keep them safe by the power of the name that you have given me. Then they will be one with each other, just as you and I are one. While I was with them, I kept them safe by the power you have given me...

'Father, I don't ask you to take my followers out of the world, but keep them safe from the evil one. They don't belong to this world, and neither do I... I am not praying just for these followers. I am also praying for everyone else who will have faith because of what my followers will say about me. I want all of them to be one with each other.'

JOHN 17:1, 6, 8–9, 11–12, 15–16, 20–21

You are better off having a friend than being all alone... If you fall, your friend can help you up. But if you fall without having a friend nearby, you are really in trouble.

ECCLESIASTES 4:9–10

You obey the law of Christ when you offer each other a helping hand.

GALATIANS 6:2

Our faith journey is an individual one, but the paradox is that to keep safe on our journey we need to stick together. Jesus knew how incredibly hard it would be to follow him on our own. Even independent Paul was to need a friend, although in his case he had to be supplied with a series of them because he was such hard work!

One of the organizations that Adrian and I admire enormously is the Prison Fellowship. They work with and pray for prisoners in many of our jails and detention centres. Their logo is a flock of geese flying in that wonderful 'V' formation we tend to associate with the RAF aerobatic team, the Red Arrows. The reason behind the choice of this logo is that on their habitual marathon flights, geese take it in turns to lead the flock, breaking the formation temporarily to let a less exhausted bird have a turn at the front. To me, this is a classic symbol of the way we as the body of Christ are intended to support each other and share responsibility.

Jesus knew how much we would need each other partly, because he helped to make us that way. We are created to be dependent beings—dependent on God and dependent on each other. That is a difficult concept for us to grasp in the 21st century. We were brought up, and we bring our children up, to believe that the aim is to move from dependence to independence and, in terms of living in the 'real' world, that is of course indisputably right. However, when we begin to suspect that what we see as the 'real world' is in fact only a tiny fraction of what God intended our world to be, we have to rethink.

Jesus also knew about our need because he became a man and experienced first-hand how terribly lonely life can be, especially when you are thought to be odd or different. Many years ago, Adrian and I worked residentially with children whom society had decided were odd and different, in a special school in Gloucestershire. Although it is now in the increasingly misty past, some of the lessons I learnt then still inform my thinking now. Often, it was in the solving of a specific problem that the learning curve was steepest. There was, however, one occasion when a solution presented itself by accident.

We were struggling. We had just taken over running our house of 'maladjusted' boys (oh, how I hated that term), and were conscious of how important it was to form a bond between them and us. Playing games and talking, especially in a circle, helped, but it was always a case of 'every man for himself', especially when they felt threatened in any way. The idea of unselfish support, of being a team player, was an alien and unwelcome concept. Adrian often said that in their games of cricket there were only two players—the batsman and the bowler. To be a fielder or to be waiting your turn to bat did not exist as a reality. It was therefore perfectly reasonable to sulk or misbehave or wander off.

One evening, a member of staff who was very knowledgeable about the local countryside told us he had discovered what he was pretty sure was a badger sett. He suggested that we took some of the boys on a night walk to see if we could find it. It was a cold night, I was tired, and I confess that I was not really pleased about being part of the coerced crowd huddled in the porch. By the grumpy looks on most of the boys' faces, I could tell that they felt much as I did. The only positive aspect, as far as most of them were concerned, was that they had got out of going to bed at the usual time.

As we crept out of the school grounds and began to ascend the nearby hill, I found my spirits lifting. It was so beautiful—so wild, so exhilarating, so peaceful.

'Miss.' An urgent voice broke into my reverie. 'Miss, I'll look after you.'

'No, I'll look after you, Miss.'

'No, I will. I'll look after you, Miss.'

Within minutes, almost every finger of my gloved hands had its own individual guardian, all of them arguing the virtues of his particular ability and right to protect me. Being out on the hills at night, I realized as I looked down, smiling ruefully, at my posse of small bodyguards, was also very, very scary.

After that, night-walking became a feature of our time in Gloucestershire. One night we squashed into an ancient burial mound at Ulay Bury, and Adrian, by flickering candle light, told a scary story, blowing the candle out on the punchline to the delighted horror of his listeners, who clutched each other and screamed enjoyably. Another night, I secretly took a small group up on the hills and hid with them in the bushes. When Adrian and his unsuspecting gang arrived on the hillside an hour later, in the mistaken belief that they had been specially chosen to go fox watching, they were greeted by flashing torches and a terrifying, whooping, hollering ambush. After their ordeal they were treated to hot chocolate, sausages and marshmallows cooked over a camping stove.

Neither of these incidents would be found in any social work textbook but on that night, as we surveyed our laughing, chattering circle of ambushed and ambushers, we knew that something good was going on. In the dark, faced with the unknown, barriers that had been erected at a very early age were at last beginning to be broken down. Surrounded by rustling darkness, we needed each other. We were keeping each other safe from danger, learning about being one with each other. Things could be said that had never been said before. Hands could be held, confidences whispered. Physical contact (sadly banned for ever now because of the danger of inappropriateness) forged bonds that no words could ever achieve.

I'd like to say that from then on there were no more quarrels and fights between the boys, no telling tales or lies, but that would be silly. It is true to say, though, that there was an increasing sense of being part of a group, even when not surrounded by darkness— of being there for each other when the chips were down—an understanding, if you like, of fellowship.

❖

Dear Father, there are times when we get so very tired of trying to get things right on our own. Help us to accept our need for those you have given to be close to us. Build our trust and break down our barriers so that we can function successfully on the long journey of life in you.

THE NEED TO SIFT

You ignore God's commands in order to follow your own teaching. And you are nothing but show-offs! Isaiah the prophet was right when he wrote that God had said,

'All of you praise me with your words, but you never really think about me. It is useless for you to worship me, when you teach rules made up by humans.'

MATTHEW 15:6–9

Jesus continued: You Pharisees and teachers are show-offs, and you're in for trouble! You give God a tenth of the spices from your garden, such as mint, dill, and cumin. Yet you neglect the more important matters of the Law, such as justice, mercy, and faithfulness. These are the important things you should have done, though you should not have left the others undone either. You blind leaders! You strain out a small fly but swallow a camel.

MATTHEW 23:23–24

Have you ever thought how incredibly difficult it is to live in a world dominated by 'spin' without being affected by it, at least to some extent? Apparently, not only should we *not* believe what we read in the newspapers but also what we are told by our elected politicians, our top scientists and indeed experts in just about every field. Again and again we are horrified to discover that there has been a cover-up, even where our safety is concerned, as in the crises of vCJD and genetically modified crops. We are so used to people in authority editing reality that the concept of 'the truth, the whole truth and nothing but the truth' seems irrelevant outside the courtroom. The truth is to be skipped around, played with or juggled, just as long as it is not told for fear of frightening or disturbing us or in any way, 'rocking the boat' of those who make decisions.

Then there is the problem of living in a society held in the grip of political correctness. Of course we needed to do something about language that had hurt and alienated vulnerable parts of society, but now, terrified to be considered sexist, ageist, racist or indeed any sort of 'ist', we are in danger of bending language into any shape that will comfortably avoid offending, challenging or, let's face it, describing other people.

No wonder we struggle with the Bible. It is unexpurgated. It has not been sexed up or watered down or airbrushed or doctored since it was first put together. It is too long, too lumpy in construction and contains a lot of bits that are so unpalatable or contradictory or offensive that as 21st-century Christians we would very much like to edit them out once and for all. It would make so much more sense if the God of the Old Testament was a little less irascible and judgmental. We'd definitely cut out some of Paul's utterances, and even Jesus could be made a bit jollier and more flexible.

Of course, church leadership has been involved in its own share of spin. Throughout history, authority figures have simply left out the bits they didn't like and majored on the bits they did. The emphasis on hell and damnation in the Victorian era has been replaced by a kind of cosy inclusivity which is in danger of accommodating just about every sin ever thought of by humanity.

Does it really matter? What's wrong with deciding to leave out parts we don't like very much or that we think will upset people? Isn't inclusivity what we want at all costs? If telling the whole truth offends or alienates, then surely it is best avoided? After all, we don't want to put people off coming to church, do we? We're struggling with numbers as it is…

Of course it matters. We cannot reduce God to bite-sized pieces that can be easily digested while on the move, or dilute him so that even babies can enjoy the taste. We must not spend so much time and money on packaging him attractively that those we persuade to 'buy into' Christianity feel let down by the contents. We ignore the sayings of Jesus that we find uncomfortable at our peril—word such as those recorded in Luke 12:49–53: 'I came to set the earth on fire, and how I wish it were already kindled! ... Do you suppose that I came to bring peace to the world? No, not peace, but division. From now on a family of five will be divided, three against two and two against three. Fathers will be against their sons, and sons against their fathers...' (GNB). The living water is not always palatable.

What we have to offer the world is the good news—not that you can be part of a cosy solution to earthly pain, but that within the grim mysteries of life you can be safe. 'Christ Jesus came into the world to save sinners' (1 Timothy 1:15)—not airbrushed sinners; just ordinary, common, grubby, unedited sinners—sinners like us.

❖

Dear Father, help us not to want to reduce everything you stand for to a size that feels comfortable for us. You are the great God of Abraham and Isaac and Jacob. You are the creator of everything good. You have given us good news that the world can never counterfeit. Don't ever let us forget your greatness and power.

SIFTING OUT FALSE 'GODS'

When we told you about the power and the return of our Lord Jesus Christ, we were not telling clever stories that someone had made up... All this makes us even more certain that what the prophets said is true. So you should pay close attention to their message, as you would to a lamp shining in some dark place... Sometimes false prophets spoke to the people of Israel. False teachers will also sneak in and speak harmful lies to you.

2 PETER 1:16, 19; 2:1

It was the night of Holy Saturday—not, you might think, an evening usually set aside for celebration, but we had decided along with friends of ours that it would be nice to be together for once, to herald Easter Sunday in much the same way that we might meet together to welcome Christ on Christmas morning.

There were ten of us—close friends from different local churches, who manage to find several excuses throughout the year to eat far too much and have a lovely time together. Some of us drink alcohol and some of us don't, but we all end up giggling and tipsy on the unlocking effect of being with people who we know love us and with whom we can be ourselves.

After an enormous meal, mellow and replete, we settled down for coffee, chocolates, drinks and chat in the living-room and, I can't remember how, the subject got round to what we imagine heaven to be like.

'For me,' said Madge, helping herself to a mint cream and

leaning back against the sofa cushions, 'the nearest I come to catching a glimpse of what I think it might be like is six o'clock in the morning when I'm out with the dogs. You know, I love being up early—unlike someone else I could mention.'

After general cheering, jeering and lifting of glasses in the direction of her husband, and much indignant protestation from him, we begged her to continue.

'It's hard to put into words. I suppose it's just that it's so still over in the woods and nothing has happened yet in the day to spoil it. It's all perfect and I can kid myself that it's just for me. Well, me and the dogs… and the birds, of course. And they are enjoying it as much as I am. Even the dew on the grass hasn't been trampled on, and every leaf of every tree looks as glossy, fresh and unspoilt as the new sun coming up. Sometimes it makes me feel so happy I could burst.'

We were all quiet, relishing the atmosphere her words had created.

'So,' she continued, 'leaving God out of the picture for a moment, I think… What? What? What have I said?' … as her attentive audience dissolved into laughter.

After her husband had pointed out to her that it was a bit much expecting God to exclude himself from his heaven just so that she could have it all to herself, the conversation moved on to other things until the clock struck twelve and we relaxed into comfortable prayer together, thanking God for giving us the resurrection of his Son.

Her words stayed with me, however. 'Leaving God out of the picture for a moment…'

Adrian and I knew Madge's God and didn't like him much. She had met him as a small child and I think it's true to say that he had disapproved of just about everything she was and did ever since. Her life as a teenager and young woman had consisted entirely of 'thou shalt not's.

Very, very gradually, through her marriage, her motherhood and her Christian friends, she had come to believe that God might just love her as she was, and the truth had begun to set her free. It didn't take much for her to retreat behind a barricade of dry 'should' and 'shouldn't' rules, however, and she always felt guilty when she was enjoying herself unless it was within an established Christian context. It seemed a jolly good idea to leave her God out of all pictures of heaven, and we were pretty sure she need not have any worries about meeting him in heaven when she got there either.

Madge's description of heaven reminded me of something Philip Yancey wrote in *Soul Survivor* about being converted from his church upbringing. He said that he crawled out of the ditch where his pharisaical church had hurled him and came back to God through romantic love, classical music and the beauty of the created universe.

In order to stay safe we must sift out wrong images of God planted in our minds by false teachers. We need courage to do so, in order that we, like Madge and Philip, might give the one true God a chance to reach us wherever and through whatever he chooses.

❖

Dear Father, we are sorry that at times we have allowed a partly false image of you to take up residence in our hearts. Please show us which parts of the image need throwing out and which are of you. Thank you for the beauty of the things you made for us—music, love, the universe. Help us to find you in them.

Flower in the crannied wall,
I pluck you out of the crannies;—
Hold you there, root and all, in my hand,
Little flower—but if I could understand
What you are, root and all, and all in all,
I should know what God and man are.
ALFRED, LORD TENNYSON, 'FLOWER IN A CRANNIED WALL'

BEWARE THE DANGER
OF THE EASY AMBLE

Jesus continued: Go in through the narrow gate. The gate to destruction is wide, and the road that leads there is easy to follow. A lot of people go through that gate.

MATTHEW 7:13

Once upon a time—I feel I can say that because this happened in the ancient days BC (before children)—I helped run a Pathfinder group in our church in Bromley. Pathfinders are aged 11–14, which is a really lovely age to work with, and the members of our group were great fun. One year we decided to take them away for a weekend of walking and fellowship, and planned a pretty strenuous hike for the second day, aiming to leave one hostel early in the morning and arrive at the second hostel by the late afternoon. Our church thought it was a lovely idea—so lovely that they decided to join us for part of the walk and bring a picnic to save us having to carry food with us.

All went well at first. We set out early and got about eight miles under our belts, stopping only for a wonderful break by an icy stream where we soaked our feet and ate chocolate and plastered our blisters. It was rough terrain and much of it was navigated in single file. There was little talking as one by one the Pathfinders decided to save their breath for the task in hand. As lunch time approached, we all congratulated ourselves on our progress and greeted parents and friends from the church with pleasure. We ate the picnic they had brought us, and then, looking at my watch, I declared that we needed to be getting on. It was at this point that the problems began.

'Oh, surely not yet,' said one mum, looking at her youngster who was stuffing his face with apple pie. 'Bless them, they look exhausted.'

'Yes, well, we do have a long way to go, so we really need to get a move on,' I said, feeling like a kill-joy as I watched families pack up their belongings with surreptitious grumblings. 'I thought we were going to have a game of French cricket or something. Not much fun for them, is it?' I heard one dad whisper loudly to his wife.

Perhaps they were right. Perhaps I had got it wrong. Maybe they were too young for such a trek. My doubts increased as I saw several of the kids who had seemed so happy earlier, moaning and complaining to their parents about how far they still had to go.

The atmosphere, when we finally parted from our support band, was not encouraging. The potent challenges of the morning that had been tackled with such excitement and commitment seemed to have been diluted by our lunch-time rest. Our pace slowed to a despondent dawdle, with mutterings of 'Never wanted to come on this pigging walk anyway' and 'Are we nearly there yet?' adding further to the gloom.

It was beginning to get dark and increasingly difficult to see the way ahead. Everyone, including me, was dispirited and tired, and the whole thing reeked of failure. Somewhat desperately I called my motley band together.

'Now, look—we can do this. We need a pace setter. Come on, David, march us into the ground,' I said—and he did. We quickened up, we began to sing and talk and forget our sore feet and at last there in the distance was our destination. There were whoops and shouts and, to my amazement, the tiredness flew away to be replaced by euphoria and a feeling of pride at a mission accomplished.

As I collapsed into an armchair and listened in amazement to an energetic game of football being played outside by the erstwhile exhausted young people, I reflected on the day.

We had only just reached our destination by nightfall and therefore placed ourselves in considerable danger, but why? The walk had been long and challenging, yes, but perfectly manageable. The reason why it had gone wrong was that we had been persuaded to slow down and relax. We had been encouraged, by nice people, to see our task as rather silly and very daunting and to feel hard done by and deprived. We had temporarily forgotten the joy of journeying with people who shared a common purpose and determination to reach their goal. The wide path had tempted us and, by contrast, the narrow way had seemed dreary and tough.

❖

Keep us safe on our journey, dear Lord. Do not let us be tempted away by well-meaning folk who have not yet caught the vision. Help us today to examine the road we are on, and to see whether we have settled for a leisurely stroll instead of the adventure you intend for us.

THEY SAID 'YES'

It is finished
Finished?
Is it?
I don't think so.
Not until the funny little woman on the Friday bus
Means more to me than I do to myself.
Not until I read aright the message of your pain-filled eyes
That I must take the ones you loved and left behind
To live with me as my responsibility.
Not until I freely place my stock of cherished certainties
Like sad surrendered weapons at your injured feet.
Not until the public and the private faces
of my troubled Christianity
Can meet, and know they recognized each other when they met.
Not until I know the names of more than half
the people in my street.
Finished?
No, I don't think so.
Not yet.

ADRIAN PLASS

(FROM *WORDS FROM THE CROSS*)

A MIXED BAG OF LOSERS

Come to see me as soon as you can. Demus loves the things of this world so much that he left me and went to Thessalonica. Crescens has gone to Galatia, and Titus has gone to Dalmatia. Only Luke has stayed with me. Mark can be very helpful to me, so please find him and bring him with you. I sent Tychicus to Ephesus. When you come, bring the coat I left at Troas with Carpus. Don't forget to bring the scrolls, especially the ones made of leather.

2 TIMOTHY 4:9–13

This passage is a quite memorable combination of the sublime and the ridiculous, isn't it? For someone like me, with a history of losing things and who has probably provided British Rail with enough umbrellas to set up a shop, it is a huge comfort to find that someone with a brain the size of Paul's could forget his coat! There's a touch of human moan here too—and a bit of intrigue. What was in the scrolls, especially the ones made of leather?

Above all, this snippet, written at the end of a letter encouraging Timothy, is an important reminder that all the writings that constitute the Bible were written by real people. Even the prophets were human beings who got up in the morning, had to do what you have to do, ate breakfast, experienced backaches and headaches and toothaches and heartaches. They, like us, struggled not only with remembering to collect up their possessions when leaving, but also with the big issues of life.

In *The Apple of His Eye* (BRF, 1996), I mentioned a youth group

I once led and how I asked them to give marks out of ten for things affecting their futures such as career, romance and so on. One category was 'adventure' and I referred to the memorable score of 'nul points' that was given by one rather timid girl. I then went on to talk about how Mary, the girl chosen to be the mother of Jesus, gave it ten when she said 'yes' to the greatest and most unpredictable adventure of all time.

Adrian and I were fortunate enough to meet David Watson shortly before he died. At the time, he was in the middle of the ghastly struggle of accepting that he might die, having been diagnosed with cancer. He was honest about the extent to which he wrestled with this most horrible of challenges, but it was beautiful to witness the peace he experienced once he had laid down his will and was able to acknowledge truthfully that 'the best is yet to come'.

This week, we are going to take time to look at some of the characters in the Old Testament who were called by God into a life of unpredictability. Not all of them were as quick off the mark as Mary, or as determined to face the challenge as David Watson, but what they had in common was that eventually they said 'yes' to the challenge God laid in front of them.

One of my favourite hymns includes the words 'such love, streaming through history'. The flow of living water has never been stemmed, despite the fact that the water carriers have been such a mixed bunch of losers! Thank goodness for Jonah—God went on using him even though he was sulking atrociously. Thank goodness for Moses who, even though it was God himself who was promising to be alongside him, still came up with a series of excuses to get out of going where he was being asked to go. Thank goodness for 'the one step forward, two step back' heroes—for the multitude of ordinary, flawed human beings whom God has used to carry out his plans, then and now.

Maybe, if we can get over our arrogance in feeling that we have to be worthy of the role, God will be able to use us to carry the water a little way towards those we know who are thirsty.

❖

Dear Father, it is so easy to say the right words but so much more difficult to mean them. Help us today to identify at least one area where we have managed to say 'yes' to your calling and one where we have not. Show us one time when we have picked up our cross, and one time when we have refused—and one time when we picked it up cheerfully enough but then made excuses to put it down when the going got tough. Guide our thoughts this week as we identify with the struggles of a few of your followers.

MOSES SAID 'YES'— RELUCTANTLY

The Lord said: My people have begged for my help, and I have seen how cruel the Egyptians are to them. Now go to the king! I am sending you to lead my people out of his country.

But Moses said, 'Who am I to go to the king and lead your people out of Egypt?' God replied, 'I will be with you…' Moses asked the Lord, 'Suppose everyone refuses to listen to my message…?'

EXODUS 3:9–12; 4:1

There is something almost comic in this famous encounter between God and Moses on Sinai.

God may be the great 'I Am', the God of Abraham, Isaac and Jacob. He may be making his first appearance for many years and doing it in spectacular fashion. He may have called Moses by name. He may be paying Moses the extraordinary compliment of choosing him to lead the children of Israel out of Egypt. He may be about to punish the very nation from which Moses is hiding and thus make him safe. He may be promising to accompany Moses personally and to back up his message with mighty miracles. But does *any* of this cut any ice with Moses? Not a bit of it!

There is no amazed expression of delight at the privilege of being chosen, no exclamations of gratitude—all Moses can see is the erstwhile murderer he knows himself to be (Exodus 2:12)—the guy who used blows instead of brains to right the wrong he saw in front of him. If he'd been God he wouldn't have chosen him, so it stood to reason that God must have got it wrong. Moses' image of himself as a loser totally obscures his vision and prompts his surprisingly churlish 'Suppose everyone refuses to listen?'

What does God do at this point? Get angry? Choose someone else? No, the creator of the universe gives him one or two very natty miracles to impress his case on the Egyptian court—a walking stick that turns into a snake and an equally impressive 'Now the hand's leprous, now it's not' trick. He even gives Moses a miracle to keep in reserve, in case the powers-that-be are still not impressed. 'Take some water from the River Nile and pour it on the ground. The water will immediately turn into blood' (Exodus 4:8–9).

Even James Bond was never equipped with an armoury like this. Yet, amazingly, this still doesn't impress our reluctant hero, who is now thinking only how his stammer will affect things. Can Moses *really* be saying at this point, 'I have never been a good speaker. I wasn't one before you spoke to me and I'm not one now. I am slow at speaking, and I can never think of what to say' (4:10)?

Surely now Jehovah will give up? Well, we probably would have done, but then we are not God. Admittedly he is beginning to sound a bit annoyed as he reminds Moses that it was actually him who made people able to speak in the first place (4:11). Admittedly there is the feel of an exasperated parent longing for a few minutes' peace and quiet in the command, 'Now go!' Admittedly we are told that God is 'irritated' when, after all this encouragement, Moses begs him to 'send someone else' (4:13–14).

Yet even now God is prepared to compromise in order to keep Moses on board. 'Take your brother along' is God's suggestion. 'I'll tell you what to say and you pass it on to Aaron' and, for good measure, 'I'll be with both of you as you speak, and I will tell each of you what to do' (4:16).

When God wants something done and has chosen one of us to do it, he doesn't give up easily, as Jonah found to his cost and salvation (see Thursday's reading).

Have you ever watched show-jumping? Have you seen how the

great riders respond to a first refusal? They don't add to their horse's panic. They gently steer their mount away from the source of failure with a pat and lots of whispered encouragement, before turning around and giving them another chance to overcome the hurdle ahead successfully.

It would seem that God too shows the same mixture of flexibility, encouragement and firmness in persuading us to go along the path he has chosen for us. Not only that, but he may even, like many a loving parent before him, give a little and allow us to take a friend along!

❖

Dear Father, we are sorry that we are so often such cowards. Moses would have been hiding in the desert for the rest of his life of you hadn't prodded him out. Please be as persistent with us as you were with him and don't let our first refusal be our only chance at the jumps you set before us.

REBEKAH SAID 'YES'— TRUSTINGLY

The servant prayed, 'You, Lord, are the God my master Abraham worships. Please keep your promise to him and let me find a wife for Isaac today…' While he was still praying, a beautiful unmarried young woman came by with a water jar on her shoulder… Rebekah walked past Abraham's servant, then went over to the well, and filled her water jar. When she started back, Abraham's servant ran to her and said, 'Please let me have a drink of water.' 'I'll be glad to,' she answered…

'Let Rebekah stay with us for a week or ten days,' [Rebekah's mother and brother] answered. 'Then she may go.' … They called her and asked, 'Are you willing to leave with this man at once?' 'Yes,' she answered.

GENESIS 24:12, 15–18, 55, 58

When I read the story of how Rebekah came to be Isaac's wife, what first strikes me is what nicely brought-up kids she and her brother Laban were.

The collection of water was one of the hardest tasks of the day for the young women of any household. The water jars were heavy and filling them took time. Rebekah had actually begun to walk back to the house where she lived with her parents and brother when the stranger, who was resting his camels nearby, asked her for a drink of water. Not only was her response spontaneous and immediate but she also offered to give his camels all the water they needed. Five camels drink a good number of water jars full of water, and we are told she went back to the well again and again until they had had enough (Genesis 24:19–20). Why? There can have been no hidden agenda in her actions. This man meant nothing to her at this point. They were simply the actions of a good, kind girl.

Discovering the stranger to be the servant of a relative was an unexpected bonus, only revealed after she had offered him hospitality in her father's home. Her confidence in her family's hospitality says a good deal about her upbringing, and Laban is equally warm in his welcome. Nothing was too much trouble for the host family. Both camels and visitors were fed and watered and made to feel at home, and all this was before they had an inkling about why the servant had come.

When they did discover his purpose, their response was immediately enthusiastic: 'The Lord has done this. We have no choice in the matter' (24:50). Presents were exchanged and the impression is that a very convivial evening was spent by one and all.

We say a lot of things over a meal and a glass or two of wine, and I don't find it at all surprising that the idea that had seemed so perfect the evening before looked less attractive in the cold light of day. Rebekah, their only daughter and sister, was to leave them, and leave them right now. I don't blame them at all for asking if perhaps she could stay for a week or so before leaving them for ever (24 :55). What I do find surprising is the trust and spirit with which Rebekah accepts her destiny. She is only a young girl. She has never met her future husband. She is going on a long journey with a man she has only known for one day. Her family would give her full backing if she decided to defer her departure, but when she is asked if she is willing to leave with this man at once she says, quite simply, 'Yes.'

People like the young Rebekah often get into terrible pickles. Sometimes others take advantage of their innocence. Their trust is sometimes abused, their generosity not repaid in kind. Their impulsiveness is sometimes foolhardy. But there is something in the young Rebekah that reminds us of another young girl in Nazareth who said 'yes' with equal trust and fervour.

Sadly, the Rebekah we meet later (Genesis 27:5–13) has lost the aura of innocent goodness that marked her out when she was young. Maybe the parental influence is no longer so apparent. Maybe life has toughened her up. Maybe she had a particularly soft spot, like many a mother before and since, for the naughtier and more difficult of her two sons. Maybe the same impulsiveness that was so attractive and right in her youth proved a weakness in adulthood, causing her to aid and abet Jacob in his stealing of his brother's birthright.

We'll never know, but I think it is fair to say that not only her father Bethuel but also her Father in heaven must have been proud of their beautiful young daughter on that special day when she welcomed a stranger with grace and said 'yes' to an unknown adventure because she trusted that it was the right thing to do.

❖

Dear Father, help us to respect the impulsive qualities you have given us as much as the more reasonable, cautious ones. We recognize that such qualities can open us to danger. We are more likely to rush in where angels fear to tread and more likely to leap before we look. We also know, however, that if we allow that side of us to have its say, we will be able to have adventures with you that the more sensible side of our personalities would frown out of existence.

So, Father, while we ask you to deliver us please from temptation today, we also ask you to give us a little more of the young Rebekah's courage, generosity and trust.

DANIEL SAID 'YES'—
BY SAYING 'NO'

Daniel made up his mind to eat and drink only what God had approved for his people to eat. And he asked the king's chief official for permission not to eat the food and wine served in the royal palace...

The other men tried to find something wrong with the way Daniel did his work for the king. But they could not accuse him of anything wrong, because he was honest and faithful and did everything he was supposed to do... They all went to the king and said: '... You should make a law forbidding anyone to pray to any god or human except you for the next thirty days. Everyone who disobeys this law must be thrown into a pit of lions...'

So King Darius made the law and had it written down. Daniel heard about the law, but when he returned home, he went upstairs and prayed in front of the window that faced Jerusalem. In the same way that he had always done, he knelt down in prayer three times a day, giving thanks to God.

DANIEL 1:8; 6:4, 6–7, 9–10

If I were asked which three images from international news footage over the last few decades have remained etched most clearly on my mind, I would probably be joined by thousands in my choices: the second plane crashing into the Twin Towers on 11 September 2001; the young girl running naked from the napalmed village during the Vietnam War; and a slight young man in a white shirt facing the might of China's armed response in 1989 in Tiananmen Square, Beijing.

That young man was just one of hundreds of idealistic Chinese students who had decided that their pro-democracy voice must be heard. He was just one of the hundreds massacred as a result. But there is something about the quiet determination of this boy, caught for ever on film, that has become an icon of still courage in the face of overwhelming moving force.

The Babylon of 597BC was easily as powerful a force in the world as China in the 20th century. It had just triumphantly captured Jerusalem, ransacked the temple of the Lord and taken prisoner hundreds of citizens of Judah (2 Kings 25:9–17). Not only that, but it was ruled by a powerful and astute leader. King Nebuchadnezzar saw that among his captives were a large number of well-educated, healthy, rich young men who could prove a source of trouble in the future. He recognized the need to get these clever young Jewish captives on his side as soon as possible. Teach them to speak and write the Babylonian language, give them the very best food and wine, train them for three years, and what have you got? A grateful élite who, instead of leading a rebellion, can help lead a country. It was brilliant strategic thinking on the king's part. How could it fail?

Easily! Nebuchadnezzar reckoned without Daniel and, indeed, without Daniel's friends. Not that you can really blame him. Daniel easily fitted into the category of the 'healthy, handsome, clever, wise and educated' (1:4) who were chosen to serve and be trained in the royal palace. Nothing on the surface set him apart, and the way of denial is unusual for dynamic, attractive young men. It is also important to remember that, at an impressionable age, these young people had good reason to be disappointed with their God.

Where had he been at the time of the devastation of their city? Why hadn't he prevented the stealing of the holy treasures from the temple, which were now being rededicated to the pagan gods of Babylon (1:2)? Was he all-powerful or was he not? Surely now what was important was survival—at any cost.

For Daniel and his friends, though, there was more to be

considered than their personal comfort and safety. For them, just as for the Chinese students, there was a principle at stake. To eat from the king of Babylon's table was to deny the only King who had ever mattered to these fervent young Jews, because it meant disobeying God's laws about 'clean' and 'unclean' food. Were they to throw away everything they had been taught to live by, simply because the weather of their circumstances had taken a change for the worse? They were not.

To Jewish believers then and now, Daniel's cheerful, calm, yet total resistance on this and other famous occasions has become a symbol of faith, courage and stoicism.

And what about us, Christians trying to live in an increasingly pagan society in the 21st century? What can we take from Daniel's story to give us strength in our resistance to the enemy? I think it is the confidence with which Daniel went about his campaign.

Take the manner in which he said 'no' to King Nebuchadnezzar's command to eat the royal food. He appears to have been charming throughout the whole episode. We are told that he asked permission not to eat the food and wine served in the royal palace and that the king's chief official was 'friendly and kind' to him (1:8–9). Daniel got people on his side. They respected him, and through him they grew to respect his God.

This was even the case for King Darius, who was tricked by his officials into having to sentence a much older Daniel to death, in chapter 6. We are told that just before throwing him into the lion's den, Darius actually said to Daniel, 'You have been faithful to your God, and I pray that he will rescue you' (6:16). Not only that, but after Daniel emerged unscathed, Darius decreed that everyone should worship the 'living God' who 'rescues people and sets them free' (6:17). It is no coincidence that during the exile in Babylon no less than two powerful kings—Nebuchadnezzar and Darius—were converted to Daniel's God.

Hitting our non-Christian work colleagues over the head with our Bibles or texting tracts to their mobiles may feel like a sortie into enemy territory but lacks a little of Daniel's expertise! We need to stand firm against the tide of popular opinion if we know it to be against what we believe is right, but we also need to remember that when doing so we represent a living God who rescues people, not a mealy-mouthed disapproving misery.

Even more to the point, when facing and resisting the unclean temptations within us, we might try doing so with a slightly more up-beat and good-humoured confidence. We have, after all, got the same God as Daniel had on our side. Perhaps then we will begin to understand in a new way what it means to move forward by standing still.

❖

Dear Father, we talk so often about wanting those close to us to know you. Help us to face the fact that Daniel brought some very influential people to you, only by taking incredible risks. We know that, for us, the chance of being literally thrown to lions is pretty remote, but help us not to mind quite so much about fitting in and being accepted. At the same time, dear Lord, point out to us when we are smug and boring. Help us to remember that we represent a living, dynamic God, and let us be proud to acknowledge you.

JONAH SAID 'YES'— GRUDGINGLY

One day the Lord told Jonah… to go to the great city of Nineveh and say to the people, 'The Lord has seen your terrible sins. You are doomed!' Instead, Jonah ran from the Lord…

The Lord sent a big fish to swallow Jonah, and Jonah was inside the fish for three days and three nights. From inside the fish, Jonah prayed to the Lord his God:

… I will offer a sacrifice to you, my Lord. I will keep my promise because you are the one with power to save.

JONAH 1:1–3, 17; 2:1, 9

When you were a child, were you ever sent to your room to 'think about what you'd done', or made to squirm for what seemed like hours outside the headteacher's study before facing possible punishment?

Well I was, even if you weren't! The lobby outside our headmistress's office had three hard chairs on which we errant teenagers awaited judgment. There was a worn dark green rug and a mind-numbing watercolour of three tall ships on the dull green wall. There was also a unique smell that I can conjure up to this day— that of the headmistress's spaniel which had a stinking cankerous ear!

Even more clear are the memories from when I was small and was banished to my room until I saw reason. I can experience to this day how my small bedroom, usually a cosy haven, felt like a lonely doom-filled prison when I was in trouble. I would enter the room defiantly shouting, fling myself sobbing on my bed, feeling hard done by, unfairly treated or just plain guilty depending on the circumstances. Then, emotions spent, I would sit miserably in the oppressive quiet, waiting for what seemed like a life sentence until my parents had decided that I had had enough time to come to my senses. I can still hear my mother's steps on the stairs as she came up to tell her repentant sinner, 'You can come down now if you are ready to say sorry.'

Having now had four children of my own, I realize that such treatment was likely to have been chosen simply because it afforded a few minutes' respite for a harrassed parent who had come within inches of murder, but at the time I was small and didn't know. What I do know is that my resolve on coming quietly downstairs was always that from now on I was going to be a very, very good girl.

I also know that this resolve lasted all of... half an hour?!

Jonah was given three days and three nights to 'think about what he'd done'. But perhaps God, like many a parent before and since, wondered in retrospect just how effective his treatment had been in the long term. While inside the fish, Jonah was prepared to offer anything in return for a way out, and certainly for a short time afterwards he is a reformed character. But had he really repented of his disobedience?

He never actually said 'sorry' to God while in solitary confine-ment. True, he did go to the Ninevites. He did pass on God's message, and Nineveh's subsequent repentance did save the city from certain destruction (3:3–10). No doubt, whenever Jonah felt like turning back, the memory of the hideous smells and sights in the belly of the big fish were sufficient to spur him on. But did he do it in good grace? He did not! We are told that after completing his task he was 'really upset and angry' and stomped off to sulk (4:1–5).

What really hits me about this story is something not so much about Jonah as about God. God will use even a sulky, silly child to work for him, because he is so filled with compassion for all of his rebellious brood. God listens to Jonah shouting, 'I knew from the very beginning that you wouldn't destroy Nineveh. You are a kind and merciful God, and you are very patient. You always show love, and you don't like to punish anyone' (4:2) and sees the outburst for what it is—nothing more than a childish tantrum. God very gently sets aside time to teach his grumpy son by means of a visual aid in the shape of a vine, just why he had asked Jonah to do what he had to do (4:6–11).

What a relief this story is to me! How often have I, as an adult, run away or stomped off from a situation where I knew full well what I should do. I've felt sorry for myself, refused to look at the full picture, enjoyed grumbling, behaved childishly, and said 'yes' grudgingly.

Can it really be true that God will still be able to use me? It looks as if he just could.

❖

Oh God, what a Father you are. We talk so easily of the 'Old Testament God' as if you were ruthless and uncaring, yet here you are putting up with rebelliousness and rudeness in order to offer the chance of salvation to 'a hundred and twenty thousand people who cannot tell right from wrong' as the story of Jonah tells us. Please, please keep putting up with us.

DAVID SAID 'YES'
TO GOD'S 'NO'

David said, 'I have disobeyed the Lord.' 'Yes, you have!' answered
Nathan. 'You showed you didn't care what the Lord wanted. He has
forgiven you, and you won't die. But your newborn son will.' … So David
went without eating to show his sorrow, and he begged God to make the
boy well. David would not sleep on his bed, but spent each night lying
on the floor. His officials stood beside him and tried to talk him into
getting up. But he would not get up or eat with them.

After the child had been sick for seven days, he died, but the officials
were afraid to tell David. They said to each other, '… He might do
something terrible.' David noticed his servants whispering, and he knew
the boy was dead… David got up off the floor; he took a bath, combed
his hair, and dressed. He went into the Lord's tent and worshipped.

2 SAMUEL 12:13–14, 16–20

What are we to make of what happened to David's newborn baby
son as a result of David's sinful affair with Bathsheba, which led him
to murder (2 Samuel 11:4, 15)? How can we ever be reconciled to
this story? I really don't know—any more than I will ever understand
why horrible things happen to innocents in any time or place. What
do we do with the overwhelming emotions that such incidents pro-
voke? David's behaviour at this crucial point in his relationship with
God might afford us one possible pathway through the pain.

For seven days and seven nights he did not cease to beg his Father

98

to give him what he wanted above all else—healing for his little son. There was absolutely no compromise in his request, no 'but if it be thy will' about his plea. Then when his baby died, despite all his pleading, David accepted God's decision absolutely and without question. Having bathed and combed his hair, he went to the Lord's tent to worship.

At the point when we badly want something, whether from our earthly or heavenly parent, we will usually offer the moon. Depending on the importance of the thing desired, our promises will range from doing the washing up for a week to being good for ever, changing our ways totally, and being for ever in debt. We coax, we plead, we verbalize our love, we are winsome and vulnerable. When we get our way, we are delightful in our gratitude.

But what about when we don't get our way? The speed with which we are capable of changing the dynamic of the relationship is almost frightening. 'Well, stuff you then!'

This is perhaps the less erudite way of expressing what many of us feel when we experience what seems to be rejection or indifference. I'm not saying that most of us will turn away for ever, but turn away we often do. Like Jonah and, on another famous occasion, Elijah (1 Kings 19:4), we go off and lick our wounds and sulk.

Many years ago, a wonderful member of our congregation was very suddenly taken ill, and on the Friday evening the church came together to pray. I will never forget what our vicar said to us. He said, 'Tonight we are not going to be brave and sensible. We know in our hearts that God knows best and we know that, when we place our brother into his hands, whatever decision God makes has to be right, but tonight we pray from our hearts and let God know what we want. Tonight we let ourselves be children.'

God's decision was just as hard to accept on that occasion as in David's case. We no more got what we wanted than he did, and there was something about the wholeheartedness of our pleading and the death of our friend the following day that, for many of us, felt like rejection. But the next morning, there we all were in church worshipping together, and together we held on to each other in faith until relational healing with God took place.

Later on, David was due to be punished again. He had insisted on counting all the people in Israel and Judah, knowing full well that it was an affront to the God who had always kept him safe, as it implied that he now relied on his army for protection (2 Samuel 24:1–9). After doing it, he felt dreadfully guilty and went to God to say sorry and to admit that what he had done was stupid and wrong. God gave him a choice of three punishments, all of them pretty dreadful. David's response? 'It's a terrible choice to make! But the Lord is kind, and I'd rather be punished by him than by anyone else.'

❖

Dear Father, we want somehow to get to the point where we can trust you even when you reject our pleas and seem to have turned your back on us. Help us to learn what David did, that whatever you decide will be the best and fairest way, because as well as being a just God you are also a kind one. Help us, like David, to submit positively to your decisions, whatever they may be.

HANNAH SAID 'YES'— AND REMEMBERED

Hannah was brokenhearted and was crying as she prayed, 'Lord All-Powerful, I am your servant, but I am so miserable! Please let me have a son. I will give him to you for as long as he lives...' Later the Lord blessed Elkanah and Hannah with a son. She named him Samuel because she had asked the Lord for him... Elkanah said, 'Stay here until it's time to stop nursing him. I'm sure the Lord will help you do what you have promised.' Hannah did not go to Shiloh until she stopped nursing Samuel.

When it was the time of year to go to Shiloh again, Hannah and Elkanah took Samuel to the Lord's house... then brought the little boy to Eli. 'Sir,' Hannah said, 'a few years ago I stood beside you and asked the Lord to give me a child. Here he is! The Lord gave me just what I asked for. Now I am giving him to the Lord.'

1 SAMUEL 1:10–11, 19–20, 23–28

Tucked away in a little village in Normandy, we and some friends own a tiny cottage. It is cosy and comfy and it doesn't have a television. While we are there, we have 'Uno' tournaments and play Scrabble and pencil-and-paper games and listen to the radio and vow, every single time, that when we get home we will change our lifestyle for good. We will cut out watching television almost entirely—we will do more jigsaws, play more board games and listen to the radio and... and what is the first thing we do every time we get home? We make a cup of tea and settle down comfortably in front of the telly to drink it!

The phenomenon of making decisions while away from home, which we break as soon as we return, should have an expression devoted to it. When I am away on a Christian conference, for example, I know exactly how I am going to change my lifestyle and that of my family for ever. The next year, I have to resolve to do it all over again—and I know that I am not unique in this sad pattern of resolutions and retractions. Otherwise, why would every gym in the country be fully signed up in January with determined slimmers and keep-fitters, and half full in February?

That is what makes Hannah so very special. Hannah is away from home when she pours out her heart to God about her child-less situation. She is at the end of her tether, having been teased cruelly by Peninnah, her husband's other wife (1:6), and is pre-pared to promise anything to God if he will only grant her desire. In fact, she promises to give back her son to the Lord if she can just be allowed to conceive. At home, she discovers to her joy that she is pregnant. When her baby boy is born, overwhelmed with joy, she happily christens him Samuel, which in Hebrew sounds a bit like 'Someone from God' or 'The name of God'.

Hannah then settles down to nurture and love her baby. A few years later, having no doubt bonded fully with her little one, she quietly and calmly sets about keeping the life-changing promise she had made all that time ago when her circumstances had been so different.

How did she do it? How did she manage to keep a promise that must have been far more costly than she could have possibly reckoned at the time she made it?

I think there are three clues. First, she gave herself a minute-by-minute reminder by calling her son Samuel. Every time she looked at her adored son, she was reminded about who had given her the chance of motherhood. Then there is the fact that she had a very supportive husband who was one hundred per cent behind her in honouring the commitment. We are told that he loved Hannah very much (1:5) and it must have been tempting for him to feel that her future happiness outweighed a past commitment. Lastly, there is the advice good old Elkanah gives her: 'I'm sure the Lord will help you do what you have promised' (1:23).

When will we get it into our heads that it is all right to be frail and fickle, just as long as we are willing to acknowledge our weakness and call on God to help us to be stronger? When will we understand that obedience to God will set us free in a way the world can never understand?

The Hannah we see praying at the temple in Shiloh, after handing over her little son into Eli's care, is very different from the distraught woman whom he first discovered, sobbing her heart out so wildly that he thought she was drunk (1:14). Because Hannah had managed to do what she knew to be right, she was confidently able to pray aloud at Shiloh:

You make me strong and happy, Lord. You rescued me. Now I can be glad and laugh at my enemies... We cannot win a victory by our own strength (2:1, 9).

Hannah's wonderful prayer is echoed in the words of Mary, many years later (Luke 1:46–55). It is interesting to speculate on just why Mary was chosen, and to wonder what was so special about her.

As I have looked this week at various people in the Bible, I find myself thinking of Mary a lot. I think about the fact that she said 'yes' to God without his promising her, as he did Moses, that he would be by her side, and without being given an armoury of miracles to ensure her safety. She said 'yes' without receiving gold earrings and promises of security and without the blessing of her family, as Rebekah had. She said 'yes' knowing that her probable fate was as grisly as that facing Daniel. She said 'yes' to the unknown without hesitation, unlike Jonah. She submitted to God's will even though she had not sinned as David had. She said 'yes' without any of the terms attached that Hannah had. Maybe that's why God chose her.

❖

Dear Father, sometimes there are things that we know you are calling us to do—things that on the surface will not bring us the happiness we think we desire. We may feel that we could never have done what Hannah did, but help us to keep her story in our minds in the same way that she kept the name of Samuel in hers. And help us to aspire to be more like Mary, who said an unequivocal, unhesitating 'Yes'.

DITCHES, DARKNESS AND DISTRACTION

(When things go wrong)

When you slept
On the cushion
In the boat
Did you dream that walk we took
You and I
One autumn afternoon
From the tiny church at Lullington
Through Littlington to Alfriston
Where ageless fields of flint and chalk
Fell seamlessly to merge and meet
With green and violet shadows
That were circling and embracing
The cathedral of the Downs?
I was in terror of a storm that day
The red and gold
Flew and fluttered round our heads
Brittle messages of loss and pain and death
The surging valley-side beyond us

Once a wild and wondrous way to rise
I suddenly discerned
Was nothing but a dumb and loveless wall
It was so sad to see familiar beauty
Now a thing of ugliness
I dropped my gaze
You spoke a word
A firm command
Into the centre of the raging storm
And when at last I raised my eyes
I saw with grateful wonder
That the splendour had returned.

ADRIAN PLASS

(FROM *NEVER MIND THE REVERSING DUCKS*)

WHEN THINGS GO WRONG

Jesus continued: I am telling you this to keep you from being afraid. You will be chased out of the Jewish meeting places. And the time will come when people will kill you and think they are doing God a favour. They will do these things because they don't know either the Father or me. I am saying this to you now, so that when the time comes, you will remember what I have said.

JOHN 16:1–4

When my thoughts were bitter and my feelings were hurt, I was as stupid as an animal; I did not understand you. Yet I always stay close to you, and you hold me by the hand. You guide me with your instruction and at the end you will receive me with honour. What else have I in heaven but you? Since I have you, what else could I want on earth? My mind and my body may grow weak, but God is my strength; he is all I ever need.

PSALM 73:21–26 (GNB)

Maybe this week is a good time for us to remember what Jesus said to the disciples so soon before he left them. It would be good to examine the costs, rewards, disappointments, temptations, challenges and joys of our walk so far. How have these things affected our energy, our enthusiasm and our efforts to keep going? Have we lost sight of our leader by running ahead, or loitering behind, or getting lost or distracted?

Sometimes we dream up grand schemes and then wonder why

God doesn't honour them. It can make us bitter and disappointed, causing us to lose confidence and doubt his love for us. This is especially the case if a group of us have believed that what we are involved with is God's will for us, and that a series of what the world might call coincidences are in fact 'God-incidences'. It is worst, of course, when prayer for healing is involved, when we have 'stood on God's promises' and had faith and been diligent in prayer, yet those prayers have not been answered. A great chasm opens up in the path before us, bringing us to a sudden stop.

Or do we feel we have got left behind? Sometimes we are left out of other people's plans. No one seems to think that we might like to be involved or even notice our existence. Everyone else seems to be striding out in some defined direction, kitted out spectacularly for whatever the journey might hold, while we trail miserably along behind in our ill-fitting plimsolls, feeling as if we might as well go home because no one would miss us if we did.

Sometimes the rejection is deliberate. Church leaders may not be in the habit of killing people who do not agree with the plans that they are convinced God has divulged to them and them alone. They can ostracize, however, and injure and abandon folk at the side of the road.

Maybe we stop moving altogether. We are exhausted and our feet hurt. We are thirsty; our mouths are dry. We've done our best and do not feel we can carry on any longer. We are not even sure if we want to. We are disillusioned or disappointed by our leader.

Or do we feel that we have been dropped into unknown territory without a map? Bereavement, loss, and other changes of circumstances can all make us feel alienated, confused, scared and ill-equipped to cope.

Some of us feel that all of these things have happened—and more. On the other hand, some of us feel fine. We are marching along in our thick, warm socks and our comfortable boots, with our backpack full of snacks, and cannot see why others are struggling. If that is you, bear in mind that you might just be in more danger of getting completely lost than all the rest of us.

Some of us fall into ditches…

It was a truly exquisite morning—cool and bright and shimmering with promise. The Cuckmere is a beautiful Sussex river but at the point where it creates a perfect oxbow lake as it meanders to the sea, it excels itself. It is a haven for wildlife and a much-loved walk for the Plass family, this particular morning represented by myself and my son, lured into an early morning stroll by the promise of a large cooked breakfast at the nearby café afterwards. By my side trotted our border collie puppy, Lucy, ears alternately flapping in the slight breeze and cocked in excitement at the new sounds of seabirds and rustling reeds. Although she didn't yet know it, today was the day when she was to be introduced to the concept of freedom with all its delights and temptations.

The moment had come. Checking for large scary dogs and speeding cyclists, I unfastened her lead for the first time. For a few minutes she remained close by, tentatively sniffing the grass, tail tucked nervously under her bottom. Then she was off, ears doing a fair impression of Piglet's in the wind as she surged across the grassy expanse, snuffling into rabbit holes, investigating promising tufts of grass and disappearing behind bushes to emerge excitedly, running back for reassurance and a quick pat before speeding away again.

Every now and then, she approached the river, shallow and divided now into small streams. They fascinated her and we watched in amusement as she cautiously crawled on her tummy down steep grassy slopes in an attempt to dip her nose in and lap the water. Several times we called her away and she came running back to be praised and petted, but the lure of the stream proved greater than her desire for our approval. It was at this moment that it happened.

Maybe the slope was too steep or too slippery, or perhaps she made a miscalculation somewhere, but as she tried to stop her front legs from skidding, her tail and hindquarters rose in the air and she flipped spectacularly over into the water. Squeaks and thrashing followed, and a very bedraggled and bewildered little dog scrambled her muddy way back up the bank, shook herself wildly and slunk over to where we were standing. She knew she had been naughty. She looked so ashamed of herself and so forlorn and so guilty that we had to laugh and cuddle her. As she looked up and saw our smiling faces, a total change came over her and she leapt up to lick our faces ecstatically with a very smelly tongue, while her wet tail wagged wildly. She was safe and we weren't cross and everything was going to be all right.

We all fall into ditches, often because we have been silly or disobedient or overcome with desire, or because we have attempted to be or do something beyond our abilities or experience. When we climb out, bedraggled and guilty, we instinctively know that there is only one way to go.

For Adam and Eve, it was to hide in the garden of Eden, away from God (Genesis 3:8). For Peter, despite the fact that he had not yet sorted out a certain matter of denying his dearest Lord, it was to leap out of a boat and run to the person who loved him most and with whom he felt totally safe (John 21:7). He too arrived wet, bedraggled and guilty. He too received a welcome he had not deserved, and I'm sure that if he had had a tail he too would have wagged it.

❖

Dear Father, you know us so well. You know that we will always do things we wish we hadn't done, and not do the things we should. Yet you still love us and are always ready to forgive us. If there is anything keeping us far from you, show us what it is today so that we can acknowledge it and come to you as Peter did.

WHEN WE WANDER FROM THE INTENDED ROUTE

The Lord said: My people, when you stood at the crossroads, I told you, 'Follow the road your ancestors took, and you will find peace.' But you refused.

JEREMIAH 6:16

The snow on Lebanon's mountains never melts away, and the streams never run dry. But you, my people, have turned from me to burn incense to worthless idols. You have left the ancient road to follow an unknown path where you stumble over idols.

JEREMIAH 18:14–15

I love the image of the 'ancient road', deeply pitted with the footprints of disciples through the ages—the path that Abraham and Moses and David and Jesus walked.

I also know how easy it is to get off the road and trot happily along some other path until stopped by an increasing feeling that it isn't the right way, that it's getting us nowhere and that in order to go forward we need to retrace our steps to the junction where we left the road. The problem we often find is that when we try to return, we discover that the true road is a long way back and has become overgrown by lack of use. It is therefore very difficult to find.

Our house is stuffed with electrical equipment—as yours probably is—but the difference between you and me is that you probably know how all yours works. I'm OK with toasters and kettles, where you just turn it on and let it do its stuff, but most of the equipment I own only ever uses a fraction of its capability. Why? Because when it arrives, I so badly want the machine to get on with doing what it does best that I don't sit down and read the manual through properly. Most functions on my microwave, for example, are a complete mystery to me, and as for my computer... well, I'll come to that later.

The thing about manuals is that pages 1 and 2 are enough for the 'baked potato' level of living. It's when we are getting into the adventurous world of soufflés and sponges that we need more in-depth information. We venture into unknown territory at our peril, as anyone who has had to clean up a whole exploded chocolate pudding from the interior of their microwave will agree. Those of us with even a modicum of common sense will know that rather than experimenting by randomly pressing knobs, we do better to hunt out the manual, go back to square one and be prepared to learn slowly, step by step.

Jeremiah, I can say with total confidence, lived in BM time (Before Microwaves or, indeed, Before Manuals). His message was much the same, however. 'Because you have left the ancient road and wandered off,' he told the people of Israel, 'you are in a muddle.' And that's where, for those of us trying to get to grips with the more complicated aspects of our spiritual lives and the constant dilemmas the world throws at us, the Bible comes in—and especially the Gospels. They are surely the manual that helps us keep our feet on that 'ancient road'. Measured against the actions and words of Jesus, many situations that seem beyond our comprehension become clear.

Oh dear! Even as I write, I know that this is so often not true. Our manual seems either too simplistic to solve the complexity of the mess we find ourselves in or very obscure or even, some might say, obtuse—rather like the manual for my computer.

I have spent many happy hours with the nice man called 'technical support' at the end of the phone, trying to sort out my muddles on the computer. Too often it is because a little knowledge has turned out to be an absolute disaster. Encouraged by the friendly little paperclip who pops up whenever I ask my computer for help, I have succeeded in completely jamming up the works on more occasions than I like to remember. Trying hamfistedly to apply Bible verses that we feel should solve whatever crisis we may be in can add to our problems in just the same way, including overlaying the problem with guilt. Thank goodness for BRF and the other organizations who know how much we need help with understanding the Bible. But what if this still doesn't seem to reach the spot? What if we still feel lost and unable to proceed?

Here's a cautionary tale: once upon a time I found that when I turned on my computer I could not access the internet. Told on screen that I was 'unable to establish a connection', supported by the fact that little arrows at the bottom right-hand side of my screen were the wrong colour and the link light on my modem was not on, I phoned my pal at technical support. In fact, I was passed from one pal to another, each one knowing exactly what the problem was... until they were proved wrong and had to pass me onwards and upwards. Each new expert asked the same string of questions, including what colour my little arrows were, and if I had tried the on-screen help package and, male pals in particular, if I had the plug in! One thing we did establish was that my PC was talking to my modem. It began to feel like marriage counselling, but I was pleased to discover that their relationship had not broken down completely!

Finally, having relaunched broadband several times without success, my arrows remaining defiantly sludgy green, it was agreed that I should have a real live engineer come to the house. Slowly and methodically he worked through his tests, establishing that my filters were adequate, there was no problem with the local exchange and that the plug was in. I was beginning to feel secure and smug. This problem was not my fault. This problem was clearly complex—worthy of a real live engineer. Finally he attached the cable from my PC to his laptop. As he was doing this he suddenly leapt from his seat and, picking up the cable, held about an inch of it between his thumbs.

'Ah,' he said.

'Yes?' I said.

'Ah,' he said again, his tone heavy with slow, head-shaking censure.

I too peered at the cable but could see nothing until I had hunted down my reading glasses. It was unbroken but there was a minuscule indentation at one point. Peering even closer, I saw that a set of tiny teeth had nipped through one wire of the cable. Do you remember that I said we had a new collie puppy?

'Ah,' I said. 'Ah.'

Sometimes even experts don't know the right questions to ask, or the right direction in which to point you. How can they? Only a close friend or a more intelligent me might have thought that the puppy could have had something to do with the problem. I only saw it when it was quite literally right in front of my nose!

Again and again, while Jesus walked this earth, his friends tried to apply their knowledge of what they believed to be his rule book. Again and again they had to learn that Jesus' response to each and every person he met involved the application of his basic rules in a new and personal way, taking into account their individual circumstances at that particular time.

❖

Dear Father, we need the manual, we need the resources, but we also need the Holy Spirit to point out when the solution to our present confusion is right in front of our nose, or to guide us back to the exact point where we departed from the road we should be on.

WHEN THE FOG COMES DOWN

Jesus told his disciples, 'For a little while you won't see me, but after a while you will see me.' They said to each other, 'What does Jesus mean by saying that for a little while we won't see him, but after a while we will see him? ... We don't know what he means.' Jesus knew that they had some questions, so he said:

You are wondering what I meant when I said that for a little while you won't see me, but after a while you will see me. I tell you for certain that you will cry and be sad, but the world will be happy. You will be sad, but later you will be happy. When a woman is about to give birth, she is in great pain. But after it is all over, she forgets the pain and is happy, because she has brought a child into the world. You are now very sad. But later I will see you, and you will be so happy that no one will be able to change the way you feel.

JOHN 16:16–22

Sometimes it is not our fault that we have lost our way. Engulfing fogs can descend very suddenly. At times like this, our vulnerability is at its height and we yearn more than anything to be able to see the way ahead clearly once more. Often we try to retreat to a place of safety, only to find that there is no way back.

On holiday in France recently, Adrian and I had a chance to visit one of our favourite places in the world, Chartres Cathedral. We had both been looking forward to the respite offered by this day, following a year in which things had gone badly wrong for almost everyone in our close family. Sitting at a rickety café table in the shadows of its great and beautiful structure, we relished the moment, over our croissants and coffee, when we would enter by the west door and look up at one of the great masterpieces of the world—the altar window depicting Mary and Child, flanked on either side by equally beautiful stained-glass creations.

'It's going to be a bit strange,' I found myself thinking. 'After all, last time we were here we were all so happy.'

Several heavy drops of rain gave me an excuse to escape from my dark thoughts, and I hurried Adrian through his last delicious flakes of pastry, scooped up our bags and coats, and together we scuttled across the square, climbed the steps and pushed open the heavy door. As we stepped into the dark, cool interior, made darker still by the grey skies outside, I almost gasped in horror. The wonderful familiar window had gone and in its place were large, bare panes of utilitarian clear glass. They looked incongruously ugly compared with the joyful exuberance of the rest of the stained-glass windows for which Chartres is world-famous. Leaving Adrian to explore, I sat down sadly in one of the small, hard chairs in the central aisle. I felt ridiculously disappointed and near to tears.

'Don't be so silly,' I told myself. 'Presumably the window has only gone somewhere to be cleaned, and what has it got to do with anything that has happened to us?' It was no good. My feelings were stronger than my will. 'Nothing stays the same; everything good and beautiful gets spoilt.'

I looked up at the window. No symbolic shaft of living light pierced the gloom. No rainbows of reflected light danced on the stone pillars. It was just plain horrid. And suddenly I was glad—glad for that gaping wound of a window, glad that my grey time was echoed even here.

Things don't stay the same, not even in such symbols of permanence as French cathedrals. Things happen—bad things, good things, hurtful things. The baby depicted in the window didn't stay a baby. He grew up and, while still a young man, he was killed, his death plunging those who loved him into a void of dull despair. All that had given their lives colour and meaning had gone. Of course we know now that it was not to last. The sun was to return to their lives in just three days, but those three days would have seemed an eternity of grey.

I knew that the window would be returned, cleaned and restored and probably glowing even more gloriously than before.

As I sat there, I felt a flutter of hope for the first time in ages. Colour would edge its way back one day into the lives of those I loved, but for now I had to accept what I could not comprehend, give my besmirched hopes and grime-coated dreams to the expert restorer and wait until he cleans them sufficiently for the sun to shine through once more.

❖

Help us to do just that today, to give our dreams and hopes and hurts and failures to you. Restore in us a clean heart, we beseech you, oh Lord.

WHEN WE RUN AHEAD

Keep me as the apple of your eye; hide me in the shadow of your wings.
PSALM 17:8 (NIV)

How priceless is your unfailing love! Both high and low among men find refuge in the shadow of your wings.
PSALM 36:7 (NIV)

Have mercy on me, O God, have mercy on me, for in you my soul takes refuge. I will take refuge in the shadow of your wings until the disaster has passed.
PSALM 57:1 (NIV)

On my bed I remember you; I think of you through the watches of the night. Because you are my help, I sing in the shadow of your wings.
PSALM 63:6–7 (NIV)

These are such comfortable words, aren't they? The image of singing away under a huge downy wing is one of soft, cosy, happy safety.

What is really important for us to remember, of course, is that when David wrote these verses he was never in a cosy safe place. He was literally on the run, fleeing from Saul, hiding in wilderness caves, fearing constantly for his very life.

In fact, the point of the 'wings' image is that he felt frightened and vulnerable and child-like and desperately wanted to be protected and safe from the big bad world that was proving too dangerous and scary for him to deal with.

Now this is David we are talking about—David who, as a boy, took a sling and a pebble and killed a giant (1 Samuel 17:48–50); David who took a harp and soothed a king (1 Samuel 16:23); David who led armies and defeated enemies. As a young hero, each and every situation provided a challenge and offered an opportunity for success. He became the darling of the nation. He no longer needed the patronage of Saul. He was doing pretty well for himself. And at that point, when he was at the height of his fame, he found himself in danger.

We see it all the time in our society, don't we? Ordinary folk who happen to have some talent or beauty become for a while extraordinary. They are picked up and nurtured by those of us who need them to alleviate the monotony of our lives. In our imaginations we turn them into more than mortals. All goes well until they begin to believe it themselves. They strut and preen and don't need us. But we're not having that! What we give, we can take back—and we do. Our manufactured pop groups are among the most vulnerable. It's as if we take a few thin, brightly coloured playing cards, build them up as high as we can, clap our hands over the beauty of what we have created, admire it for a while and blow it down when we get bored with it.

So it was with Saul. He had loved and nurtured his little hero until the fateful day when, we are told, the crowds welcomed the hero back from war by chanting, 'Saul has killed a thousand enemies; David has killed ten thousand enemies!' (1 Samuel 18:7). What he had given, he could take away—and he did. It started a chain reaction which led to David having to break ties with his greatest friend, Jonathan, and hide from the very people who had once adored him. The lion killer was now the prey being hunted down.

The gutter press is well named, as it spends so much time sniffing out the many who have fallen into gutters. We know a lot about what happens to our fallen heroes. We see close-ups of faces bewildered and hurt and scarred by the kicking they have received, faces so desperate to be the nation's darling again that they will plead and beg to be placed back on the pedestal from which they have fallen. They will do anything, be anything—reinvent themselves if necessary. We still prefer to devour the juicy bits, chew the entrails and eventually kick over the carcass of our fallen prey.

Some survive—those who have self-awareness, those who have good friends and those who seek refuge in the right place. They go home, close the doors and let their mums tell them, over a nice cup of tea, what silly fools they've been to believe all that nonsense. David has chosen the way of survival. He is seeking refuge in the right place, acknowledging that only God, owner of the wings under which he wants to hide, could fight his battles for him.

Sometimes we run ahead of God. We begin to believe that we don't really need him, that we are invincible in our own right, that what we do must succeed because our past experiences show that. We believe it when others flatter us. In fact, sometimes, when things are going well, we forget that we need protecting at all. In other words, at the times when everything feels safest and calmest, we put ourselves at greatest danger.

The image of the wings is echoed in the cry of Jesus when he looks upon Jerusalem and despairs. 'I have often wanted to gather your people, as a hen gathers her chicks under her wings.' Jesus continues by saying, 'But you wouldn't let me. And now your temple will be deserted. You won't see me again until you say, "Blessed is the one who comes in the name of the Lord"' (Matthew 23:37–39).

The people of Israel no longer felt they needed God's protection, and they had therefore put themselves in peril. Maybe today is the day of reckoning for us. This could be the day when we say, 'I have run ahead. I have been too quick to believe what others say. I have put myself in danger. But now I want to come back—back under the shadow of your wing, back to where I am a helpless child again, back to the place where I can safely and confidently sing, "Blessed is the one who comes in the name of the Lord."'

❖

Does this image ring true for you? Have there been times when you have felt so close to God that you have experienced a comfort almost like a safety blanket around you? If so, where and when have you felt closest to God? Is it when you experience his creation? Is it when you are alone? Or is it through those you love?

Allow your imagination and memories to help you draw close to him now. You are safe; you are loved; you are home. Open the door and come in. What will make you feel clean again? What hurts need unburdening? What anger are you bursting to express?

Take this precious time to talk through with God whatever is on your mind and in your heart. And whatever you do, don't edit it before submitting it to him!

WHEN THE STORMS COME

Anyone who comes and listens to me and obeys me is like someone who dug down deep and built a house on solid rock. When the flood came and the river rushed against the house it was built so well that it didn't even shake. But anyone who hears what I say and doesn't obey me is like someone whose house wasn't built on solid rock. As soon as the river rushed against that house, it was smashed to pieces!

LUKE 6:47–49

We all experience storms in our lives. At least, I think we all do. One particular year, it never seemed to stop pelting down on my family, and the weatherproofing of my faith took a mighty battering. I rarely slept through the night, and at three o'clock one morning I crept out of our bedroom and went and sat on the stairs and howled out to God. How could he have let all this happen to us? What had I done? I was in grave danger of equating the battering we were getting with God's disapproval.

Perhaps I had built my faith house so flimsily that it was going to be smashed to pieces. Perhaps I had heard his word and disobeyed it, and that was why we were in danger of collapsing in the storms.

I must have sobbed my fears and hurts and pain out at last because I remember huddling there and feeling totally spent of energy and belief and courage. Then I remembered something— something that happened when I was a little girl.

My father was a loving man but, like many fathers of his

generation, not a demonstrative one. For a touchy-feely child like me, that presented quite a problem. I longed for him to cuddle me but that was not his way. There was an exception to his undemonstrative norm, but it required a particular set of circumstances to bring it about. First it had to be raining. Then it had to be evening. It was best when it was winter.

You see, every evening my father and I walked our dog round the block before I went to bed. It was usually a rather boring event—my father silent, far away in his thoughts, as remote as ever. Our dog would be far away as well, running ahead of us, her whole being absorbed in enjoyably snuffling at the heightened scents of the evening. I often wished I also could be elsewhere—preferably at home, watching television. But when it was dark and pelting with rain, my father took his enormous black umbrella with us and tucked my arm tightly into his as we battled our way round our familiar route. From under the rim of the umbrella I could see the rain splashing into puddles by the light of the street-lamps. I could feel Cindy's wet tail and warm breath reassuringly close as she was held on a very tight rein. I could hear the rain drum-thudding on the skin of the umbrella and I would skip to its rhythm, so snug and so safe and so protected did I feel—almost as snug and safe as a duckling tucked under its mother's waterproofed wings, waiting for the rain to pass. As we saw yesterday, David too discovered that, wonderful as his easy childhood relationship with God had been, there were special blessings to be experienced when forced to take shelter under his father's umbrella.

When the sun is shining, there is no need to seek refuge and it is easy to forget that there can be anything to be said for rainy weather. During our year of storms, I found I was umbrella-walking with God a good deal of the time. Although part of me longed for the beauty and peace of calm skies, part of me realized that I had been given a special sense of what being safe in God really means. But then didn't Paul say that 'in all things God works for the good of those who love him'? (Romans 8:28, NIV).

❖

Dear Father, help us to understand in a new way that however battered we are being by the storms right now, we will survive because we are safe in the only way that really matters, under the umbrella of your love. Lead us to discover the unique blessing of closeness that you have available for each one of us when times are epecially ghastly.

WHEN THE ROAD AHEAD
IS BLOCKED

Do you really love life? Do you want to be happy? Then stop saying cruel things and stop telling lies. Give up your evil ways and do right, as you find and follow the road that leads to peace.
1 PETER 3:10–11

Sometimes we know all too well what is blocking our way—something that we can't get round, can't get over, and can't rise above. Knowing what the problem is, however, doesn't mean that we can bring about a solution, does it?

We are walking along a mountain path. In front of us is a landslide. Beside it, the ground cuts away, revealing a drop of 30 feet. What we need is a bulldozer. Then we would be able to get past—but we haven't actually thought to bring one with us...

So it is with sin, and especially with forgiveness. We know what we need to do in order to remove or reduce the obstacle in our way. We just don't happen to have the equipment in our backpack to do it.

The truth is that one of the biggest differences between us and God is that we are hopelessly incapable at the art of forgiving our enemies. Maybe that is why Jesus homes in on this charactistic in the only prayer he gives us: 'Forgive our sins, as we forgive everyone who has done wrong to us' (Luke 11:4). Then, in the Sermon on the Mount, Jesus tells us to pray for those who ill-treat us (Matthew

5:44), and demonstrates this himself from the cross with the words, 'Father, forgive these people: they don't know what they're doing' (Luke 23:34).

This is at the heart of our salvation both then, in Jesus dying for us, and now, as we seek daily renewing and cleansing in order to move forward. Unforgiveness holds us back like no other sin. It drags our thoughts into dark muddy places where hate and revenge lurk in the shadows. It is the devil's best ally, and he ensures it remains strong through a diet of hurting memories and angry impotence. He knows that our inability to overcome what we know to be a sin will keep us turned away from the only one who can help us, sapping our energy in our determination to manage on our own, and possibly even causing us to give up altogether.

When Adrian and I were in Bangladesh on behalf of World Vision, we visited a large number of different projects in the city slums and were surprised by how varied they were. Why did some communities receive funding only for health centres and baby clinics while others had schools and some even advocacy programmes and teenage training schemes? It was explained to us that the community itself determines what is its first priority. In an area where babies are dying regularly because there are no trained midwives, no schemes for innoculation and no understanding of basic cleanliness and nutrition, there is little point in building a school. The first priority is to keep infants alive, and when basic health care provision is in place the next stage can be considered. It is the same with praying for forgiveness for our enemies.

We may have said the words, may even have embraced our enemy but we know in our heart that there is nothing actually there. It's like pretending to give a gift of a wonderful flower in a flowerpot when in fact we know we are holding a pot containing nothing but earth.

We have to go right back to basics. Do we have within our soul the tiniest seed of desire for the person who has sinned against us to be forgiven by God and by ourselves? If we have, then we ask God to nurture and water that seed. If we haven't, then we have to ask for the tiny seed to be planted before we can do anything else. We can't make the flower appear by force of will or by pretending.

In other words, we first have to cry out to God for help in the midst of our sin, then we have to allow ourselves to accept his love and forgiveness of us, and gradually, when we are secure in this, we can move on to asking for a miracle, the divine softening of our hearts so that we desire to forgive those who have done us wrong.

As Portia says in *The Merchant of Venice*:

> *The quality of mercy is not strain'd,*
> *It droppeth as the gentle rain from heaven*
> *Upon the place beneath.*

Shakespeare was such a clever old thing, wasn't he? Portia goes on to say, 'It is twice blest: It blesseth him that gives and him that takes'—and that is why God sees it as something we should seek with all our hearts. It is as vital to our healthy life as our daily bread, and should be sought with equal zest and energy. But it is even more than something that we need to do to remain spiritually healthy. In a world where the emphasis is always on protecting individual rights, not yielding them, there is an active power in the act of forgiveness.

As Dostoevsky wrote, in *The Brothers Karamazov*:

At some thoughts one stands perplexed—especially at the sight of men's sin—and wonders whether one should use force or humble love. Always decide to use humble love. If you resolve on that, once and for all, you may subdue the world. Loving humility is marvellously strong, the strongest of all things, and there is nothing else like it.

Gandhi, too, had much to teach us about the strength and power of forgiveness. He once said, 'An eye for an eye makes the whole world blind.' His peaceful non-co-operative reaction to injustice could never be seen as weak, involving as it did courage and commitment and personal suffering. The effect, however, was remarkable. Lord Mountbatten, viceroy of India in the turbulent 1940s, wrote, 'On my Western front I have 100,000 crack troops and unstoppable bloodshed. On my East I have one old man and no bloodshed.'

Powerful, indeed! Forgiveness is a regular bulldozer, fit to remove mountains or at least reduce them to rubble that we can scramble over.

❖

Dear Father, unlock those parts of us where bitter thoughts and hurts have been stored away. Unblock our thinking, and free up the channels where forgiveness should be flowing freely. We want to move forward but without your help in these areas we are helpless.

WHEN THE WAY AHEAD LOOKS TEDIOUS

The Lord gives strength to those who are weary. Even young people get tired, then stumble and fall. But those who trust the Lord will find new strength. They will be strong like eagles soaring upward on wings; they will walk and run without getting tired.

ISAIAH 40:29–31

Don't get tired of helping others. You will be rewarded when the time is right, if you don't give up.

GALATIANS 6:9

Sometimes it is not that we are incapable of moving forward because of the size of the obstacle, but just that we are daunted by the prospect of plodding along a way that has become monotonously predictable. It seems dreary, boring, unendingly the same.

When my boys were small, we moved house, and this meant that they had a long and tedious walk to school every day. They and I dreaded it and they moaned and complained all the way to school until I decided that something needed to be done. I became a master inventor of ways to make the road seem shorter, like guessing how many paces it would take to get to the next tree or lamp post or gate, and then seeing which of us had made the best guess as we loudly chanted our steps one by one. We told stories in rounds, one line each, or, when we came to the long upward slope that seemed endless and tiring, pretended that we were pulling ourselves up a mountain on a rope. Hand over hand they would groan and splutter as they pulled themselves up the 'steep' incline and then they would cheer and leap about, to the surprise of passing motorists, when they reached the 'summit'.

The walk home was the time when I would hear all their news, good and bad, plus the most recent playground gossip which, needless to say, when coming from primary classes, was not very juicy but often very intriguing. The boring everyday slog to school became for them—and, I have to confess, for me as well—a quality time which I missed when they grew old enough to walk to school on their own.

As Christians we've been taught the value of regular disciplined prayer. And sometimes we find it easy to experience the poetry of God's quiet presence. Sometimes God himself can feel almost tangible and very real. Sometimes the comfort of familiar surroundings liberates us or gives us solace as we pray. There is strength in the simplicity of knowing that all you need to do to talk to God is close the door of your room and stand in the presence of your Father, who knows what you want even before you say it.

But sometimes (and I meet an awful lot of people who say 'most of the time'), it isn't like that at all. Prayer feels like a dismal, boring, miserable expedition towards a place we feel we never reach, so we don't bother to go there more than we can help, and we wonder why we feel so lacking in energy, so defeated.

One of the important things about acquiring a puppy is that they need walks—lots of walks. The cost of not taking Lucy out is a day of madness, chewed shoes, destroyed patience and most of the contents of her so-called 'heavy duty' dog bed being distributed throughout the house.

So we take her. We may not feel like it, but we do. And every time we go out, I reflect on the fact that what started as duty has become a pleasure as the smells and sights of the nearby countryside have entered our daily routine. You forget, you see. If you don't walk, you lose touch with all that is most precious about the world God has made.

'Huh!' I can hear you say. 'You must have got your puppy in the summer. What about the freezing mornings and the sloshing muddy trenches of the winter? What about the swishing tail of a filthy soaking dog when they return from such a walk, and the unique smell of wet dog that permeates every room and is definitely an aroma you would not recommend to someone trying to sell their house?'

I know, I know. But at least it's real, it's tangible, it's earthy. At least it has a smell. Increasingly I am finding that as a result I am having quality time with God, either talking to him, simply enjoying his presence or battling something out with him, sometimes shouting or singing or crying when the wind and weather are noisy enough.

I'm not suggesting that all Christians should buy dogs just to energize their quiet times, but at this particular time it has prevented my spiritual life from going as pear-shaped as a puppy-ridden house.

In *Colours of Survival* (Zondervan, 2000), the book Adrian and I wrote after our World Vision travels, I mention a street-girl project we visited in Hazarabagh, a slum on the edge of Dhaka. It has come to be a parable of exactly what I am talking about here.

The people running the project were working with little girls who had no concept of 'normal'. They had no idea that being a child could involve having the right to say 'no' to abuse—no concept of self-worth or self-respect. How could they, when they smelt and looked horrible with their filthy tangled hair and running sores, and when they could see how different they were from the rich children who passed them by in their rickshaws?

The two women in charge hit on a plan to help the children value themselves sufficiently to turn away from the life of prostitution which is the only career path immediately available to girls on the streets of Bangladesh. They decided that every morning when the girls arrived from the street, they would wash their hair and put on a nice, brightly coloured dress.

'They feel pretty,' one of the women told us. 'They look at each other and feel happy. They see that they too are special, they too are children. And it is in this good mood that they go to their lessons and play their games and learn to sew and eat their tiffin and sing songs.'

She went on to say that they have to take off the 'nice dresses' at the end of the day to prevent them being stolen when they return to the streets, but 'the next day they come again, and the next, and they will begin to want to be clean and to like the feeling of smelling good. And when they get older—about eleven—they will want to learn a trade so that they can continue to wear a nice dress, and because they will have a value for themselves they will think they do not want to be a prostitute.'

❖

Dear Father, we can't bring about the actual change but, like the men with their lame friend who cut a hole in the roof to lower him down to meet Jesus and be healed, we can use our imaginations and talents to discover new and effective ways to reach you. Help us to open our minds and hearts and imaginations to you so that you can work creatively within us for your glory.

FOOD AND REST FOR TIRED TRAVELLERS

(The promises of God)

How is it possible to be so many things?
Success and failure sit within my life like children on a double swing
One takes me high and then the other
Once I dreamed of swinging high enough to see the tops of tallest
towers
But I have had enough of swinging now
I want to take the swing down from the bough
And sit out on the lawn and watch the flowers
I would settle happily for peaceful sunshine days
A little gentle praise
A smile that passes softly now and then between the two of us
A single glance that knows and understands
Can something of this nature be arranged?
Father, grant me sense and strength enough
to place my spirit in your hands
Or I must swing until a chain breaks
No more failure, no success, no swings
And me a broken victim of these unimportant things.

ADRIAN PLASS

(FROM *WORDS FROM THE CROSS*)

TIME TO STOP

You, Lord, are my shepherd. I will never be in need. You let me rest in fields of green grass. You lead me to streams of peaceful water, and you refresh my life.

You are true to your name, and you lead me along the right paths. I may walk through valleys as dark as death, but I won't be afraid. You are with me, and your shepherd's rod makes me feel safe.

PSALM 23:1–4

Jesus said: If you are tired of carrying heavy burdens, come to me and I will give you rest.

MATTHEW 11:28

I would like you, if you will, to take a little time to think about the familiar words of the 23rd Psalm. I want you to imagine you have in front of you a map plotting your spiritual journey with the Shepherd. now allow your mind to take you back to when you first started your journey. Put an imaginary 'I woz here' sticker on your map.

Now I want you to try to picture hwere you are in respect to the Shepherd now—not where you were a few months ago or where you hope to be in a few months' time, once you've sorted yourself out and got back on track, but now, today. The only right answer is the honest one. Put an imaginary 'Red marks the spot' sticker on your map.

You see, I meet lots of people who began their spiritual journey hoping for an immediate close walk with their leader but who, for a long time, have felt that they were trailing miles behind and now feel that they are beginning to catch up. I also meet many who began striding out confidently behind their Lord but somehow feel that they have been left behind. Only you will know where you in respect to the good Shepherd.

So are you still walking close behind, as you were at the start—or closer still? If not, at what point did you become separated? What caused that separation? Do you feel you are operating in your own strength? Have you deliberately left the Shepherd for some reason?

Are you still hearing and responding to his voice, or have you got bogged down or tangled up by what life is throwing at you? Are you too tired or frustrated to listen? Or have you fallen into a ditch because you've followed the wrong voice?

Do you even feel confident that you could recognize his voice if you heard it? Do you feel that he is not bothering to communicate with you? Or even that he has let you down, or let his world down? In other words, have you decided to stop listening out for him?

Do some of these things apply, if not to you then to those you love?

Have you been trying really hard to struggle along behind your guide, and now feel resentful that you have tried for so long to keep to the narrow way and got little joy from the experience? Maybe you need an opportunity to tell him how disappointed and angry and let down you feel.

Or perhaps you are just plain exhausted, and you simply need to stretch out by the peaceful river and relax in the warmth of God's love. That can be easier said than done, of course! Many a marriage runs into problems as soon as husband and wife get to spend quantity as well as quality time together—for example, on holiday. They expect to be happily and uncomplicatedly renewed and refreshed, but discover instead that even though they have been living under the same roof, their ways have diverged and there is a huge distance between them. This applies to all relationships, of course, not just to marriage. Taking time out of the normal routine together can therefore be scary. Things may need to be said. Tears may need to be shed, and feelings shared. We may need to rediscover how to laugh. Forgiveness may need to be sought. But creating a space together can be an opportunity to see how to retrace steps to the point when the paths first separated, and can offer a chance to resolve to strike out again together.

This applies to our relationship with God, too. There may be things we haven't said to him for a long time, that need saying before we can relax in his presence. Deliberately seeking quality time with him will give us a chance to shed those necessary tears, to express our feelings, to laugh, to seek his forgiveness and to plan together the best way to continue our journey. We are told constantly that his love is there for the asking and now might just be the time to ask.

This week we are going to take a little 'green pasture' time out. We are going to seek renewal and refreshment. We'll take off our backpacks, stretch out on a grassy knoll, remove our boots, paddle our blistered feet in the stream and drink from the living springs of his promises for us.

Dear Father, we want to spend time in your presence this week not straining to find answers or agonizing over our guilt or striving to find a way forward. We want to be renewed and refreshed. Some of us need to sort out some things with you, but especially we want to relax in your love and gain strength and nourishment from the time with you. We are not very good at it. Most of us haven't a clue how to relax with you. Show us how, dear Lord.

HE SEES WHEN WE DO OUR BEST AND WHEN WE FAIL

Jesus continued: When you pray, go into a room alone and close the door. Pray to your Father in private. He knows what is done in private, and he will reward you. When you pray, don't talk on and on as people do who don't know God. They think God likes to hear long prayers. Don't be like them. Your Father knows what you need before you ask.

MATTHEW 6:6–8

Jesus understands every weakness of ours, because he was tempted in every way that we are. But he did not sin! So whenever we are in need, we should come bravely before the throne of our merciful God. There we will be treated with undeserved kindness, and we will find help.

HEBREWS 4:15–16

Isn't parental pride a beautiful thing to witness? I don't mean the gloating, selfish pride of pushy parents who are fulfilling their own frustrated dreams or who are blind to their children's faults. I mean the sheer joy that parents feel when they are watching the culmination of what they know to be the result of hard work, commitment and sometimes sacrifice on the part of their children.

I saw it at the finals of Wimbledon recently when the champion's parents, having sat in nail-biting, restrained silence through four sets of tense drama on the Centre Court, danced like lunatic

Muppets when the match was over. I saw it when I sat in a crowded hall and watched over 400 young doctors graduate from medical school, and felt my brother and sister-in-law nearly burst with quiet pride as my niece walked across the stage to receive her congratulatory handshake. And, in a tiny hut in one of the poorest rural communities in the world, during our trip to Bangladesh on behalf of World Vision, I saw it in the face of another parent of another girl. Surrounded by a group of women, including her mother, grandmother and several aunts, none of whom had had the privilege of any education whatsoever, Sima Rai, eleven years old and glowing with the responsibility of the task, wrote her name laboriously in our somewhat shabby little notebook. Proud sighs, tongue clicking, and shaking of amazed heads were only surpassed by the beaming face of her mother lifted to mine, confident of my appreciation of her daughter's massive achievement. It is one of my most beautiful memories, surpassing even those of that afternoon when my niece graduated, and where excellence was also celebrated.

I've seen it somewhere else as well—at a junior school sports day when one sturdy little five-year-old girl displayed a different kind of excellence. Her potato must have been the wrong shape for her spoon! It seemed to bounce off as soon as it touched the metal, but every time it happened she ran after the potato, picked it up, replaced it with minute care and carried on determinedly, tongue between teeth in an expression of fierce concentration. Long after the rest of the children had finished and rushed laughing to join their team-mates, she plodded solemnly on and, of course, received rapturous applause from the spectators when she finally crossed the finishing line.

But how would she feel? Coming last is horrid, especially when you are small. Her expression, when she turned to her mum, told me everything I wanted to know about her upbringing. She knew she would see, as indeed she did, pride and joy at her determination and courage.

When Jesus taught us how to pray, he referred to a Father who 'knows what is done in private'. The sheer slog, the setbacks, the loneliness and cost of our walk along the way are seen by our Father. He knows every inch of our journey, and what more can we ever ask but his pleasure with us at those times when we try our best, and his celebration with us in our special moments.

❖

Dear Father, can this be true? Are you pleased with us when we do our best? Do you really understand how difficult we find it to keep in the race sometimes—how much we long to give up?

Father, give us confidence today to bring to you not only the areas of our lives where we are failing but also those where we might just be doing OK. And help us to feel your smile.

WE ARE ALLOWED
TO BE REAL

Be humble in the presence of God's mighty power, and he will honour you when the time comes. God cares for you, so turn all your worries over to him.

1 PETER 5:6–7

My friends, the blood of Jesus gives us courage to enter the most holy place by a new way that leads to life! ... We have a great high priest who is in charge of God's house. So let's come near God with pure hearts and a confidence that comes from having faith.

HEBREWS 10:19–22

We have a space in our morning family service at church when anyone in the congregation can share their news. When our minister began this, it was rather stilted. 'News time' consisted of birthdays, serious illnesses and deaths and that was about all. As we grew more confident that what mattered to us might just matter to our church family, we began to share a little more of what was on our hearts. Children's exam results, house moving, the problems of those close to us, and answers to prayer formed the bulk of the allotted time. Rarely was our minister fazed by the contributions until a few weeks ago. Several people had shared news, including myself, as I gave an update on my mother's recovery from a broken hip.

'Anyone else before we bow our heads in prayer?' One hand shot up. It was that of the minister's own six-year-old son sitting in the front row. What news could his little lad possibly have to share with the whole church? It definitely wasn't his birthday. No one in the family was ill. No pets had died. Surely he couldn't have forgotten his and his wife's own wedding anniversary?

Puzzled, he asked his little boy what he had to share. Adam stood and, to give his news the weight he clearly felt it deserved, turned to make his announcement to the whole congregation. He took a deep breath. 'Yesterday...' he paused for dramatic effect before proceeding solemnly, 'yesterday, I rode my bicycle without stabilizers.' There was a pause. Fortunately the congregation responded appropriately to the import of the moment and applauded generously as his dad ruefully pointed out that he could vouch for this achievement as his own feet had the bruises to prove it, where Adam had run over them.

At coffee time after church Adam came up to me. He and I are pretty good friends. 'Did you hear my news, Bridget? You know, about the stabilizers?'

'Yes, Adam, I did. Thank you for sharing it with us.'

Adam nodded in satisfaction, one news-bearing member of the congregation to another, before rushing off to join the rest of his biscuit-guzzling gang.

If Adam had shared his idea of what he was going to contribute with his dad at breakfast, it is conceivable that he might have been told that perhaps this wasn't quite the sort of news that fitted the slot. After all, if everyone did the same...

Thank goodness he didn't. We bandy the words 'church family' about pretty lightly, don't we? If we really want it to work in the way that Jesus, and Paul after him, hoped it would, we have to think a bit about what 'family' means to us.

To me it means coming home. Home is where you crash through the door to pour out the day's news to someone who cares about every bit of it—someone who rejoices and whoops with you over your gold star, so modestly received in public, who cuddles away your pain over the hurts you have accumulated during your day.

Someone to whom you know you can bring the whole unedited version of your experiences and feelings.

The rabbi and broadcaster Lionel Blue said something a while ago that affected Adrian and me deeply. He said, 'Judaism is my home, not my religion.' It reminded me of the words of another Jewish writer, Jonathan Magonet, who, in a book called *Returning* (Bloch, 1997), wrote these wonderful words:

> *And when at close of crimson nights and frenzied days*
> *You'll writhe in darkness and will struggle in a maze*
> *Of demon's toils, with ashes strewn upon your head,*
> *And lead shot blood, and quicksand for your feet to tread.*
> *The silent house of God will stand in silent glade.*
> *It will not chide, or blame, or scoff, will not upbraid,*
> *And none will beckon you and none repel with stern*
> *Rebuke. For upon the threshold Love will wait to bless*
> *And heal your bleeding wound and soothe your sore distress.*

Is that how we feel about our faith, based as it is on our relationship with God? Maybe it depends on the confidence we have in that relationship.

King David clearly felt that he was at home when he came to God with his questions and requests. We like the psalms, don't we? They comfort and uphold us. They form part of the backbone strength of our worship and praise. They remind us of our frailty and God's permanence and power. They are good in wedding and funeral services. But have you ever thought about how we edit them constantly? When did you last hear in a church service any of the bits where David asks God if he would mind throwing his enemies into 'the deepest pit' or some other very unpleasant place? Take Psalm 58:6–9, for example.

> *Shatter their teeth.*
> *Snatch out their fangs.*
> *Make them disappear like leaking water,*
> *and make their arrows miss.*

Let them dry up like snails
or be like a child that dies
before seeing the sun.
Wipe them out quicker
than a pot can be heated
by setting thorns on fire.

Of course there are good reasons for not reading out these parts in church. They are hardly relevant or edifying, but there is a danger in ignoring them every time. We should remember that David did not edit his thoughts when he came to God, because he didn't think he had to. The disappointment and the anger went where they should. He knew that his Father would want to hear everything, not just the worthier sentiments. He didn't have to pretend to be more or less than he was. What mattered to David would matter to the one who loved him. In the middle of anything life threw at him, he was safe in the arms of one who would have the wisdom to sift out the parts that needed ministering to, those that needed reprimanding and those that needed encouragement.

We have not quite got as far as David in our church 'news time' but maybe one day we will. Our disappointment and anger need to go where they should, and we need to believe—as our minister's son and David did—that if something matters to us, it matters to those who care about us and it matters to God.

❖

Dear Father, give us the confidence that David had. Help us to remember that only through confrontation will we find truth and healing, and only through sharing will we find space for growth. Let us be ourselves with you, just as we are with our families—free to express whatever we are feeling and thinking.

HE CAN DO ANYTHING

In a large house some dishes are made of gold or silver, while others are made of wood or clay. Some of these are special, and others are not. That's how it is with people. The ones who stop doing evil and make themselves pure will become special. Their lives will be holy and pleasing to their Master, and they will be able to do all kinds of good deeds.

Run from temptations that capture young people. Always do the right thing. Be faithful, loving, and easy to get along with. Worship with people whose hearts are pure. Stay away from stupid and senseless arguments. These only lead to trouble, and God's servants must not be troublemakers. They must be kind to everyone, and they must be good teachers and very patient.

Be humble when you correct people who oppose you. Perhaps God will lead them to turn to him and learn the truth. They have been trapped by the devil, and he makes them obey him, but God may help them escape.

2 TIMOTHY 2:20–26

What if I could speak all languages of humans and of angels? If I did not love others, I would be nothing more than a noisy gong or a clanging cymbal.

1 CORINTHIANS 13:1

A woman once approached Adrian after he had spoken at a church meeting and severely took him to task. She told him she had stopped reading his books because of something derogatory he had said about Jesus. As Jesus is the centre of his life and has been since he first became a Christian at the age of 16, he was understandably puzzled. He may have said derogatory things about just about everything else connected with the church but not about Jesus!

'Well, you did,' she went on. 'You said that Jesus was the pits and...'

'Hang on a minute. I would never have said that. Just let me think...'

'You said it, and I've thrown away all your books and...'

Understanding dawned. 'I've got it. It was in *Alien at St Wilfreds*. Mmm. What I actually said was that, in the great motor race of life, Jesus is the pits.'

Most of us do much the same thing with this passage from 2 Timothy. We stop reading after the third sentence because we think we know what the conclusion will be. 'Some of these are special, and others are not. That's how it is with people.' Well, that probably confirms everything we've ever thought about ourselves, doesn't it? We know which pots we are—wood or clay, definitely. We can think of lots of gold and silver pots. They shine away every Sunday—talented, dynamic, beautiful, zany, organized, in fact everything and anything we think we are not.

How dangerous! Not just for those of us who feel wooden and clay-like but also for the more gilded among us. It's dangerous because the *next* sentence is the crucial one here: 'The ones who stop doing evil and make themselves pure will become special.'

I was once part of a huge Christian celebration where the quality of the worship was out of this world—an excellent band fronted by a fantastic leader supported by hundreds of people singing their hearts out. One of the songs we were singing included the beautiful words 'Let me be a sweet, sweet sound in your ear.' I was singing away at the top of my voice with everyone else. Suddenly I felt a chill surround my heart. There were things going on behind the scenes at this celebration, which I and many others there knew about, and which were wrong—really wrong. I stopped singing and stood there, listening to the glorious waves of sound reverberating through the hall, knowing that we were in fact making a horrible sound in God's ear.

God has always made it clear that what will make us gold and silver in his eyes is our efforts to be good—our attempts to stop doing evil, to make ourselves pure.

Even as we think the words, most of us know we will fail. We can no more turn real wood and clay into gold and silver than stop doing evil and make ourselves pure. If we take a trip down to the potter's shop that we read about in Jeremiah, however, and observe the potter working at the wheel, we can hear for ourselves the good news. 'The pot he was shaping from the clay was marred in his hands; so the potter formed it into another pot, shaping it as seemed best to him' (Jeremiah 18:4, NIV). There's no suggestion of the potter saying, 'Sort yourself out, clean yourself up and come back when you're attractive enough to be in my shop!'

As long as we are attempting to perform a sort of character liposuction on ourselves in order to make ourselves more beautiful and acceptable, we are wasting valuable time. God wants to call us and needs to use us. He can't do that if we have our heads down, trying to pummel ourselves into a better shape or a prettier colour. Strangely enough, the only way to 'make ourselves pure', special and beautiful, is to accept ourselves as we are, admit that we're bound to fail, and then hand ourselves over to God, the potter, so that he can do whatever is necessary to make us less evil and more pure.

I once met a couple who had got themselves involved with the ghastly pyramid-selling schemes that swept Britain in the 1980s. In order to motivate yourself into working and selling even more, you were encouraged to cover your walls with pictures of what you would buy with the money you were hoping to earn—the car, the house, the holiday. You repeated like a mantra that you could do this, achieve more, become the best, acquire what you wanted to acquire.

In terms of our relationship with God, what he wants is the opposite of this. He wants us to hold up in front of ourselves true likenesses of what we are. We need to admit that we are still the same old sinners but that we want to be different. We actually want to be transfigured, to be good, to be comfortable in our skin, to be useful. We need to look to the future, not to see what can be poured into our lives but to see how we can be poured out.

❖

Do you believe that God, the potter, loves the unique clay creation that is you? What kind of pot would you like to be? How would you like to be used? Do you dare be reshaped or redecorated? Dare you trust yourself in the hands of your Father-creator? Taking risks is never easy but he won't begin a remould without your permission!

Offer yourself to God to be turned into any shape he chooses—or left as you are. Spend a few minutes acknowledging what is unique in you and allowing the possibility that the things you hate about yourself can be transfigured.

It's a nice thought, isn't it? Your pot can be placed in the royal dresser to be used when needed for the glory of God!

HE WILL GIVE YOU ANOTHER CHANCE

People of Jerusalem, you don't need to cry any more. The Lord is kind, and as soon as he hears your cries for help, he will come. The Lord has given you trouble and sorrow as your food and drink. But now you will again see the Lord, your teacher, and he will guide you. Whether you turn to the right or to the left, you will hear a voice saying, 'This is the road! Now follow it.'

ISAIAH 30:19–21

People of Israel, you are my servant, so remember all of this. Israel, I created you... Turn back to me! I have rescued you and swept away your sins as though they were clouds.

ISAIAH 44:21–22

Our human fathers correct us for a short time, and they do it as they think best. But God corrects us for our own good, because he wants us to be holy, as he is. It is never fun to be corrected. In fact, at the time, it is always painful. But if we learn to obey by being corrected, we will do right and live at peace. Now stand up straight! Stop your knees from shaking and walk a straight path. Then lame people will be healed, instead of getting worse.

HEBREWS 12:10–13

As promises go, the one in Isaiah 30:19 is special, isn't it? It's the same promise contained in the story of the prodigal son, who is met by his father before he has even reached home (Luke 15:20). All God is waiting for is our call for help, and he will be there as soon as he hears it. All we have to do is admit we have gone wrong and our sins will be swept away (Isaiah 44:22).

So why do we find it so hard to believe? After all, we live in a world where second chances are the norm. Famous person falls publicly from grace. Famous person is vilified by the media. Famous person cries on television. Famous person is accepted back. But is famous person forgiven, or is famous person only reinstated so that we can watch and wait for them to fall again—and this time further and with far less chance of returning?

This travesty of forgiveness and the opportunity to start again is our media-drenched society's horrible 'set to fail' alternative to God's promise.

God, Isaiah 44 tells us, has swept away our sins as though they were clouds. I like this picture very much. When I was a child growing up in Norfolk, Saturdays often meant a trip to the seaside in my grandpa's car. As this was before seat belt regulations, there seemed nothing wrong in an arrangement where six people squeezed into a car designed for four. My special place was on the floor of the front seat, squashed against my nana's knees. We were an optimistic family weatherwise, so often when we set off, egg sandwiches in the boot, it would be under dreary grey skies, and anyone who knows Norfolk knows that that's a lot of sky we're talking about. But always my nana, knowing how strongly the winds can blow in that area of the country, would say comfortingly, 'We just need enough blue to make a Dutchman a pair of trousers and we'll be all right.'

I would peer expectantly through the tiny corner of window that I could actually see and eventually we might be rewarded by at least enough blue to make a very diminutive Dutchman some extremely skimpy trousers. Sure enough, by the time we arrived at the sea, the grey clouds would often have been gusted away to exist no more, replaced by fluffy puffy white ones floating in blue—the type Pooh Bear eulogized over. Blue is such an invigorating colour, so suggestive of being happy again! Everything seems possible when the sun comes out from behind the clouds.

The woman caught in the act of adultery believed she could start again when she was told to go and sin no more (John 8:11). Matthew believed he could change when Jesus called him away from his counting desk (Matthew 9:9).

Often, even when we want to give people a fresh start, we are unable to rid our minds of how they have failed in the past. Can we believe or trust them again when they promise that this time everything will be different? When they do fail again, we shake our heads and tell ourselves we could see it coming, we are not surprised, they never fooled us. We parents know how easily we fall into this trap with our children, however hard we try. And as for trusting ourselves, we know from past experience of our weaknesses that our chances are slim—and maybe it is better to be realistic and acknowledge that so far we have only seen enough hopeful blue to make a tiny pair of trousers instead of enough to clothe the whole of Holland's male population...

The power of God's belief in us is so much mightier than ours, however. He may choose to correct us, as any good parent would, and it won't feel much fun at the time, but because he is God our past sins, however heinous, can be wafted away, never to exist again. Not only that but, having disposed effectively with the grey mass that has so depressed and confused us, he can firmly set us off once again in the right direction under a blue sky.

Remember the words from Hebrews and Isaiah at the start of today's reading: 'Stand up straight! Stop your knees from shaking and walk a straight path.' 'This is the road! Now follow it.'

❖

Dear Father, help us to learn from your parenting of us to confront but also to forgive—absolutely, completely and optimistically—so that we bestow a second chance as generously as you do.

THE PEACE OF GOD THAT PASSES ALL UNDERSTANDING

Always be glad because of the Lord! I will say it again: be glad. Always be gentle with others. The Lord will soon be here. Don't worry about anything, but pray about everything. With thankful hearts offer up your prayers and requests to God. Then, because you belong to Christ Jesus, God will bless you with peace that no one can completely understand. And this peace will control the way you think and feel.

PHILIPPIANS 4:4–7

Sometimes we feel like giving up, don't we? It's all very well ploughing through dark vales when we feel confident that our leader knows what he is doing and where he is going, but sometimes even this is open to doubt.

When things go wrong for us, there is a real temptation to feel ashamed of God. I can think of several situations when I have felt that if I'd been God I would have done it differently and enabled people to avoid unnecessary pain. This applies especially to children, doesn't it? Whatever happened to the idea of guardian angels in the case of children like Holly and Jessica, murdered in Soham, or Sarah Payne in Sussex? Our anger and unhappiness can mean that we feel almost ashamed of God, in the way that we feel ashamed of members of our family when they let us down. We say things like, 'How do you expect people to believe in you when you…'

There are many dangers at this point for us, and we all react differently. Some of us scurry into the safety of our castles, lower the portcullis and harden our attitudes to the 'dreadful sinners' outside the walls, separating ourselves from evil. It makes us feel more in control. We firm up the rules about who is in and who is out, and to anyone who doesn't fit exactly we deny the benefit of the doubt. It is safer that way. We don't care if it means that we are likely to exclude all who see the world differently from us—the poets, the prophets, the lateral thinkers, those whose are sick and disturbed, those who make us feel uncomfortable. This is a total misinterpretation of the good news that Christ Jesus came into the world to save sinners. We need to acknowledge the fact that Jesus referred to all of us as sinners, and that, by contrast with God's goodness, between us and the worst paedophile or Saddam Hussein there is but a sliver of an inch.

Most of us, possibly for many of the same reasons as Peter's in the courtyard (Mark 16:66–72), know what it feels like to deny God's importance in our lives to those who challenge us. We feel isolated by our beliefs, threatened and confused, and our own safety, at that exact point in time, feels of paramount importance. Perhaps at that moment, God, instead of being someone we are immensely proud to be associated with, appears weak and in-effectual. Maybe we just want to be accepted, part of the 'in group' relaxing round the fire. Maybe we convince ourselves that it isn't really denial, just expediency. We can so easily put ourselves into the guilt-induced danger of living with our backs turned to the source of light and joy and healing. Thank goodness he doesn't turn his back on us!

Others of us are tempted to forget that Jesus never said that we would have immunity from the diseases that erupt from our sin-driven world, or from natural disaster, although he did promise us something wonderful. His promise is that we have access to something the world does not have. If we try to be gentle and turn to God in prayer in the middle of whatever is going on, we discover a peace that makes no sense in the circumstances. That peace will control the way we think and feel, and can help those we come in contact with, sometimes even turning sinners into saints.

❖

Dear Father, thank you for reminding us that we have direct access to you at all times. Thank you that you are the source of something the world cannot give and cannot take away, something we desire above everything—peace.

NOTHING CAN SEPARATE US FROM HIS LOVE

If God is on our side, can anyone be against us? God did not keep back his own Son, but he gave him for us. If God did this, won't he freely give us everything else? If God says his chosen ones are acceptable to him, can anyone bring charges against them? Or can anyone condemn them? No indeed! Christ died and was raised to life, and now he is at God's right side, speaking to him for us. Can anything separate us from the love of Christ? Can trouble, suffering, and hard times, or hunger and nakedness, or danger and death? ... In everything we have won more than a victory because of Christ who loves us. I am sure that nothing can separate us from God's love—not life or death, not angels or spirits, not the present or the future, and not powers above or powers below. Nothing in all creation can separate us from God's love for us in Christ Jesus our Lord!

ROMANS 8:31–35, 37–39

I will lead the blind on roads they have never known; I will guide them on paths they have never travelled. Their road is dark and rough, but I will give light to keep them from stumbling. This is my solemn promise.

ISAIAH 42:16

I, the Lord, was ready to answer even those who were not asking and to be found by those who were not searching.

ISAIAH 65:1

This is quite a claim that Paul is making in Romans, isn't it? Nothing—nothing—absolutely nothing can separate us from God's love for us in Christ Jesus our Lord.

Do you know about the old 17th-century philosophical chestnut, 'I think, therfore I am'? Not surprisingly, much convoluted thinking grew from this statement by Descartes, culminating in an international debate over whether an external object (for example, a chair) actually exists when no one is observing it. I was intrigued by this, especially when I learnt that one philosopher's view was that even when no human being is looking at the chair, God himself is still looking at it—so, yes, it will still exist.

So it is with the love of God. We can wonder and worry all we like about whether God really exists and loves us, or whether it is just in our minds and imaginations, but Paul says that it doesn't matter. God will go on doing it anyway.

That is not the same as saying that nothing can separate us from God, because of course we can separate ourselves from him by our own choice. We can turn our back on him. We can leave him out of our lives, deny his presence in our past and deny his place in our future—deny his very existence.

I know many parents who are sad. Their children may be doing very well in their careers and their marriages and their social lives but, despite the foundations laid in Sunday school and church, they have not found God relevant to their world as they have grown up. Often in their teens they jogged happily off along a path of their choosing without even a backward glance to their heavenly Father, and when they were so far away that they could no longer see him, he ceased to exist as far as they were concerned. These parents love their children just as much as they ever did, but so often they are crushed with guilt, dreading the worst question ever invented in Christian circles: 'Are your children going along with the Lord?'

Paul tells us that this means very little in the grand scheme of things. God is love whether we are in relationship with him or not, whether we have ceased to believe in him or not. Jesus, who, when he was living on earth, was love personified, died for us whether we would have been standing by the cross or jeering in the crowd. And we are told this by Paul, who had marched energetically down a certain path, totally convinced that he was going the right way, until ambushed by God on the Damascus road, that day when Paul was journeying, with time to think, time to reflect on Stephen's extraordinary words as he died, time to see the martyr's shining face in his mind (Acts 7:55–56; 9:1–5).

The good news for us in Isaiah 65:1 is that God is unceasingly seeking out those whom he loves, even if they are not looking for him.

❖

Today, as we try to rest in God, let us confess our sins to him—not our failure to keep our children on the 'straight and narrow' or to convince others we love of the relevance of God to their lives, but our sin of doubting his love for all his children, his power to forgive us and his knowledge of when and where is the right time to ambush us with his love.

THE NARROWEST RAVINE

On that day his father turned from him
For in his sacred heart
He headed up the holocaust
Perpetrated endless petty meannesses
On Sunday afternoons in Peckham Rye
Murdered frightened children on the moors
Didn't give the mower back
Calmly supervised the killing fields
Cheated British Rail
He watched the blank-eyed starving babies die
And sulked because there was no ginger ale
Perfect circles
Do not think they end
Do not think they start
Think only that he holds us all
Within his sacred heart.

ADRIAN PLASS

(FROM *WORDS FROM THE CROSS*)

THE WAY IN

When Jesus was setting off down the Mount of Olives, his large crowd of disciples were happy and praised God because of all the miracles they had seen... When Jesus came closer and could see Jerusalem, he cried and said:

Today your people don't know what will bring them peace! ... Jerusalem, the time will come when your enemies will build walls around you to attack you... Not one stone in your buildings will be left on top of another. This will happen because you did not see that God had come to save you.

LUKE 19:37, 41–44

To interpret the day when Jesus rode into Jerusalem as a nice jolly day, completely at variance with what was to happen later in the week, is to take this event badly out of its context.

It is, without doubt, a day of rejoicing. For a few hours Jesus deliberately allows himself to be honoured as the coming Messiah—the eagerly awaited king predicted in Zechariah 9:9. In fact, he carefully manufactures his entrance on an unridden colt, to the delight of the thronging spectators, who were familiar with the scriptures, especially those pertaining to the coming of the Messiah. He does not rebuke the euphoric crowd any more than he dismissed the blind beggar who had addressed him as the Son of David (Mark 10:47). So palm branches, a national symbol of victory for the Jews, are waved. Even jubilant cries of 'Hosanna', which means 'Give salvation now', are allowed. Indeed Jesus himself tells the angry Pharisees outside the gates of Jerusalem that if there was any attempt to stop the cheering the very stones would cry out in protest (Luke 19:40).

Yes, it is a day of celebration for the gleeful subjects, but what of the king himself?

It has been a very long journey from Galilee to Jerusalem. It has also been an exciting one for the growing crowd of fellow pilgrims accompanying him. They have seen spectacular miracles—lepers healed, a blind man's sight restored and even a man brought back from the dead. They have heard stories that delighted them with their irreverence for the teachers of the law, and enjoyed the conversion of Zacchaeus. They have praised God for what they have witnessed and approached Jerusalem increasingly confident that the firework display of power they have already seen will be as nothing compared to what will happen when their leader gets to the holy city.

Their growing excitement is paralleled by what must have been increasing despair and sadness in Jesus. There is clearly no rejoicing in his heart as he watches the seeds he sows fall on stony ground. Repeatedly en route Jesus tried to emphasize what the coming of the kingdom would really be like, but no one wanted to know.

When some of the Pharisees who witnessed the healing of the ten lepers asked Jesus when God's kingdom would come, he answered, 'God's kingdom isn't something you can see' (Luke 17:20). When women brought their children to him to be blessed, he used the opportunity to make the point that unless we become like children we will never enter the kingdom of God (Luke 18:17). To the crowd who 'thought that God's kingdom would soon appear', he told a long story, the point of which was that nothing was going to happen in a hurry (Luke 19:11–26).

None of this dinted the conviction among his expanding mass of followers that something dramatic was to occur on arriving in Jerusalem. They were sure that Jesus was about to be crowned King of the Jews and the Gentile intruders would be vanquished.

Even his disciples didn't understand. And, let's be honest, there was nothing vague or obscure in the way Jesus spelt out what was to happen to him once they arrived in Jerusalem. 'Everything that the prophets wrote about the Son of Man will happen there. He will be handed over to foreigners, who will make fun of him, ill-treat him, and spit on him. They will beat him and kill him, but three days later he will rise to life' (Luke 18:31–33).

Why? Why did no one understand? Why did even his closest followers persist in their belief that Jesus was going to behave in a certain prescribed way? I think it is because they really thought they *knew*. Brought up on the scriptures, they knew what the Messiah would be like. They were sure they knew what he would do. It was one of those 'cherished certainties' that they had securely packed away. Everything that Jesus said had to fit somehow into that package of certainty. If it didn't, it could be thrown out or reinterpreted.

No wonder Jesus wept as he came down the Mount of Olives and caught his first glimpse of the city where his life would come to an end. He wasn't weeping for himself, however. He wept for us.

He wept for all of us who have been blinded by what we think we *know* to be right—and who, as a consequence, have allowed ourselves to be led into ditches by blind leaders; and for those of us who, seduced by promises that we can have the riches of the kingdom *now*, have wandered from the way in pursuit.

He wept for those of us who will experience the destruction of our dreams and expectations because we have hardened our hearts and closed our eyes and minds to the truth.

He wept for those of us who have chosen death over life, and for all who wanted and still want their way, their truth and their life and will therefore always reject the Jesus who continues to weep over them.

❖

Dear Father, would we have understood? Would we have been blinded by our own expectations? Like your followers, we want so much from you, dear Lord, and we want it now. Help us today to see where we have allowed cataracts to build up and cloud our mind's eye. Bring us back to the way, the truth and the life.

FACING LOSING
EVERYTHING

Jesus said: Now I am deeply troubled, and I don't know what to say. But I must not ask my Father to keep me from this time of suffering. In fact, I came into the world to suffer.

JOHN 12:27

Jesus said, '… It's easier for a camel to go through the eye of a needle than for a rich man to get into God's kingdom.'

LUKE 18:25

Jesus was a very, very rich man. The eye of the needle he was being asked to get through was the finest ever created. No door has ever been made narrower.

It was going to involve shedding every fragment of what he had acquired while here on earth. The things that stirred his senses— the good and bad smells, the sounds, tastes and sights that flavoured his world as they do ours. The challenges and confrontations that sharpened his wits and inspired his imagination. Meals round tables with friends and wine and candlelight. The joy of communicating, of storytelling, and even the frustration when he knew he had not got across the truth he was expounding. Solitude and crowds. Sleep and waking, walking and talking. The ability to make a difference to people's lives in a way that no other person could. The privilege of serving those he loved. Perhaps, above all, the heightened understanding only he could have of *shalom*—experiencing in the midst of whatever was happening the peace that only his Father could bestow.

It all added up to life—a life that he was as loath to turn his back on as any of us would be.

Of course, much of what he was going to relinquish voluntarily is familiar to those of us who have become imprisoned by ill-health or failure. The chance to wake in the morning and wonder 'What am I going to do today?' The choosing of clothing and food and activities. The enjoyment of anticipating, of hope for the future and shared memories of the past.

Some would say, 'At least Jesus was able to make a choice. That choice has been taken from me.'

Jesus was going to be betrayed and abandoned by almost all of his friends. Many of us too know what it is to be stabbed in the back, even if not so literally as Julius Caesar. Divorce and bereavement create chasms of loneliness and bitterness which only those going through them can begin to understand and, for many, such loss proves to be a life sentence. For Jesus it would only be a few days.

He was going to have to live with the fact that those who cared for him would not understand why he was doing what he was doing, and some who had admired him would begin to doubt him, despise him and turn their backs on him. Well, standing up for what we believe to be right has always been a bit of a lonely road.

Jesus was going to experience the torture of sleep deprivation. At the risk of minimizing the agony of sleeplessness, most mothers and fathers know something of that feeling.

Jesus was going to lose all dignity and feel degraded and humiliated. Old age, with its breaking down of control over basic bodily functions, is equally cruel and unpleasant. Even the bravest and most stoical members of our older generations can be reduced to tears of humiliation when they are forced to be cleaned up and padded like babies.

Jesus would be at the mercy of people who would see him as no more than a temporary toy to play with and discard. But that is no more than the fate of many Jews in concentration camps during the Second World War, or citizens of more recent tyrannical regimes, and nothing compared to the demise of children at the hands of paedophiles whose plan is abuse and murder.

Jesus was going to feel the guilt of having sinned. Let's face it, we all know what that feels like, to a greater or lesser degree—to wake feeling hot with shame, to see hurt and bewilderment in those we have let down. There's nothing unique here in Jesus' experience.

He was going to lay down his life for thousands whom he had never met, yet even such heroism has been shown by ordinary men and women, especially during times of war.

He was going to be tortured, experience terrible pain and die in agony. So? Almost all of us can think of someone we care about who has endured such an end. Terminal illnesses have a nasty habit of becoming aggressively brutal, taking no prisoners, torturing dying bodies until the very last breath is breathed.

But none of us—not one—has lived our life in the knowledge that that suffering is the reason we are here. None of us has experienced the full combination of all and more of these horrific deprivations in the space of a few days. And not one of us—and at last I can speak with total assurance—has been asked to move from being God incarnate to Sin personified, holding within one frail body the whole world's rebellion against God.

This week we are going to follow the agonizing choices our dear Lord made in the last week of his life—knowing that they were all made for us.

❖

Dear Lord, we are going to find it hard to accept the enormity of your gift to us, as bit by bit we pick up and examine what you discarded for our sake. Such generosity is too overwhelming and we are going to find ourselves wondering whether there could really have been no other way.

Help us to keep in mind Guz and his fellow pilgrims, whom we met at the very start of Lent. This is the door that you couldn't walk around, climb over or slide under. You had to go through it, knowing that on the other side there would be life in abundance.

THE NARROWING PATH

It was before Passover, and Jesus knew that the time had come for him to leave this world and to return to the Father.
JOHN 13:1

The Jesus we meet in Jerusalem is almost frightening in his single-mindedness as he sets up the stage where the last scenes of his life will be played out. He knows that time is not on his side. After three years of exhausting inspirational work, he has just three days left—only three days to pass on to his friends the urgent information about how they can stay physically and spiritually safe when he has gone. He also has only three days to alienate himself from all but his most loyal followers. He has arrived in Jerusalem on a wave of approval, which must crash and disperse if the ultimate divine plan is to be completed.

There are to be no more signs and wonders in the crowded streets. No more response to the immediate need of some ordinary individual, which will require a change in direction or a time-delay. No more quizzical eyebrow-raising at the ridiculous challenges laid before him by teachers of the law. No more laughter with his friends as he deliberately flouts the man-made Sabbath laws of the Pharisees and strolls through the fields chewing on straws of forbidden wheat. There are to be no more whimsical, witty stories delivered on sunny hillsides to captive audiences who will ponder and debate the meaning of the teaching at their leisure.

The final days of teaching and healing will take place in the temple, thus making sure that his audience is limited. The nature of the stories themselves will have changed. The light is soon to be extinguished, but at this moment it is on full beam, shining into corners, uncomfortably illuminating good and evil with a clarity never seen before. His stories will emphasize that there is to be no compromise: wickedness will be punished, and God will not tolerate selfishness or pride or even foolishness.

This is Jesus the artist, painting his last pictures with more graphic darkness than ever before. Just as the anti-smoking and anti-drink/ driving campaigners use increasingly stark and grim images to show that their message involves choosing between life and certain death, so too does Jesus. The stories he tells in the temple end with the villains being 'smashed to pieces', 'thrown outside into darkness', 'crying and gritting their teeth in pain', having the doors closed against them, 'punished for ever' (Luke 20:18; Matthew 24—25).

For those who had only heard of his reputation as a teacher and healer who brought life to everything with which he came in contact, the man they encountered during this festive time must have been at least a disappointment. I can imagine the whispers beginning: 'Not a great asset to the celebrations, this Jesus... Can't see what all the fuss was about... Downright miserable, if you ask me.'

Then there are his dealings with the traders in the city, who must have traditionally looked on Passover as a nice little earner. Where is the Jesus who called Matthew from his desk and Zacchaeus from his tree—the Jesus who offered sinners salvation and hope and belief in their ability to change their ways? Those who witnessed his violent hurling of stall owners out of the temple must have been shocked (Matthew 21:12). Admittedly these men had habitually taken advantage of innocent folk who just wanted to get it right when they came to the temple, by buying doves or pairs of pigeons to please their Lord.

That's what you do at Passover in Jerusalem, though. You have to save up all year. It's part of the tradition. No need to get that worked up about it! Who does this man think he is?

During these last three days, Jesus seems to have set about

deliberately goading the teachers of the law into finally determining that he must die. In doing so, he must have further alienated himself from many pilgrims to the city. Was there any need to go quite so far in antagonizing the religious leaders? Previously it would have been rather fun listening in to the verbal duels—fencing with protected foils, as it were—but now? How do the onlookers feel as they hear him accusing the Pharisees of locking people out of the kingdom of heaven and making their converts twice as fit for hell as they are? He is insulting them publicly, every hit finding its mark: 'You're like tombs that have been white-washed... full of bones and filth... You are nothing but snakes and the children of snakes!' (Matthew 23:14–15, 27, 33).

There is one more thing that Jesus must do. During these last public days of freedom, he must put in place the means of his own demise. He knows that the chief priest and nation's leaders are aware that they cannot arrest him and have him put to death during Passover, for fear of the people rioting. They need an inside accomplice. Did Jesus himself set out to provide one? Did he lavishly condone Mary's extravagant and apparently wasteful gesture of pouring precious perfume over his feet, in order to infuriate his treasurer Judas to the point where he would decide to betray his leader? (John 12:1–5).

The path ahead is narrowing. The last gate is in sight. Escape routes will soon be blocked by a crowd increasingly vulnerable to the temptation that is to come. There is just time for one more essential event to take place behind the scenes—a meal with friends.

❖

Jesus, at any moment you could have stopped it all. Your followers loved you. They would have kept you safe from harm. Jerusalem could have been yours. Instead you deliberately turned off the light and let darkness take control—for us.

SAYING GOODBYE

Jesus... had always loved his followers in this world, and he loved them to the very end...

Jesus... knew that the Father had given him complete power. So during the meal Jesus got up, removed his outer garment, and wrapped a towel around his waist. He put some water into a large bowl. Then he began washing his disciples' feet and drying them with the towel he was wearing. But when he came to Simon Peter, that disciple asked, 'Lord, are you going to wash my feet?' Jesus answered, 'You don't really know what I am doing, but later you will understand.'

'You will never wash my feet!' Peter replied. 'If I don't wash you,' Jesus told him, 'you don't really belong to me.' Peter said, 'Lord, don't wash just my feet. Wash my hands and my head.'

JOHN 13:1, 3–9

The last night Jesus spends in private with his friends is overwhelmingly sad.

I wonder how Peter and John felt as they prepared the foods that were used as part of the traditional meal celebrating the escape of the children of Israel from slavery in Egypt. The dishes of bitter herbs and salt water were symbols of their suffering and tears, and the burnt lamb shank reminded them of the time when, by daubing the blood of the lamb on their doors, they were kept safe from the angel of death who passed over and killed the firstborn in every Egyptian household.

What an ironic contrast there was between the triumph of

heavenly intervention the disciples were celebrating and their own circumstances. Fear must have hung in the air—bewilderment too, and maybe a sense of failure. Only a few days before, the city had been at their master's feet. Now the band that had marched with such pride throughout Galilee was in hiding, furtively sharing together the Passover meal at a secret venue of which only Jesus knew the whereabouts beforehand.

For Jesus, as he knelt before his embarrassed followers to wash their feet, the pain must have been agonizing. Giving up your status and reputation is one thing; giving up your friends is quite another, especially when you know that without you they will fall and fail. The disciples never had been able to understand what he was getting at unless he spelled it out to them, and often not even then! This live demonstration of the fact that he was deliberately going to give up all the power bestowed on him, and that godly leadership would always involve service, was a case in point. There goes Peter, feathers ruffled as usual, vehement in his protests. Then, as soon as he feels he has understood what his Lord is doing, he capitulates totally and with good humour. Poor, dear, loyal Peter, who is to fail his master so devastatingly in just a few hours' time!

What did Jesus feel as he held up the bread and then the wine and asked them to remember him in the future whenever they broke bread together? We will never know, but I think it is fair to assume that the suffering that will dominate the days ahead has begun. Certainly we are told that Jesus is deeply troubled as he says the words, 'One of you will betray me' (John 13:21).

Of course he knows who it will be, but it must have cost him dearly to see the shock and fear in the faces of his friends, folk with whom he had spent quantity and quality time for three years. Understanding the battle raging in Judas, curbing the power within himself that could have brought Judas back into the fold, maybe even preventing any possible lapse in his own resolve, Jesus moves the situation a step further. 'Judas, go quickly and do what you have to do' (13:27).

His plan now firmly in place, there seems to be a relaxation of tension. As if he has all the time in the world, Jesus gently re-inforces his teaching about the importance of love and service. How clearly John remembers and records the words of Jesus that night in chapters 14—16 of his Gospel.

Jesus is going ahead but will prepare a place for them, and one day they will all be together again. He is the vine, the truth, the way. He is not going to leave them like orphans: he will be back. He has to go, because otherwise the Holy Spirit will not be able to come. On and on he goes, warming them with his promises, with the last rays of his dying sun.

Think of his prayers: 'Keep them safe by the power of the name that you have given me... I don't ask you to take my followers out of the world, but keep them safe from the evil one' (John 17:11, 15). These are prayers full of love and concern, not for himself but for those he cared about.

Then Jesus gets up and together they cross the Kidron valley and enter a garden on the Mount of Olives, the garden where they have been to pray every evening since coming to Jerusalem—the garden where Judas will know where to find him (John 18:1–2).

❖

Jesus, we will never know what it cost you as a man to go through that last evening with your friends. Help us to come alongside your suffering in our imaginations today. Give us a deeper understanding of what it cost you to give your friends away.

THE LAST BATTLE

Jesus went with his disciples to a place called Gethsemane. When they got there, he told them, 'Sit here while I go over there and pray.' Jesus took along Peter and the two brothers, James and John. He was very sad and troubled, and he said to them, 'I am so sad that I feel as if I am dying. Stay here and keep awake with me.'

MATTHEW 26:36–38

It is in the garden of Gethsemane that Jesus enters his greatest battle. He has given up status and power and entrusted his friends into the hands of his Father. Now he has to surrender his will.

Even now Jesus knows that, as he puts it later, he only has to ask his Father and 'straight away he would send me more than twelve armies of angels' (Matthew 26:53). That is a luxury denied us, but it is clear that it is also an irrelevance to him. It is purely as a man that he must move forward now. The eye of the needle is still too small, the gate ahead of him still too narrow. There are more riches to be jettisoned and only he can do it.

It is a sign of Jesus' increasing human frailty that he is not sure he can do it alone. Never has he expressed the need for his closest friends more clearly than during the short time they are together in the garden of Gethsemane. He is clearly weakened by the emotional tensions of the evening, exhausted and desperately vulnerable, but they too are utterly worn out. They have nothing left to give. The poignancy of the little remembered conversations must have come back to haunt Peter and John and James. Maybe if they had known that those would be the last conversations they would have with him... but of course they didn't know.

Maybe this is as it should have been. Only acceptance, by the human Jesus, of the nightmare ahead would secure the freedom of the world's prisoners, defeat death and unlock the gates of heaven.

The fact that it is to be harrowing is evident in his struggle. He calls out to his Father with heartbreaking desperation, 'My Father, if it is possible, don't make me suffer by making me drink from this cup.' Silence. 'But do what you want, and not what I want' (26:39).

His Father is not there for him. His friends are not there for him either. Utterly alone in the darkness, he calls out for a second time and again drives himself to the same point of accepting his fate... and again... three times.

Finally the battle is won. We are told that Jesus returns for the last time to his sleeping disciples and, with a new calm, says to them, 'The time has come for the Son of Man to be handed over to sinners. Get up! Let's go. The one who will betray me is already here' (26:45–46).

Jesus knew exactly what he was agreeing to. As a direct result of Jesus' surrendering of his will, every other human dignity will be torn from him. During the next 24 hours he will be played with like a toy, stripped and humiliated, tortured, mocked, spat on and beaten, and he will be alone. Not one of his friends will have acquired enough faith from their time with the light of the world to ensure they don't stumble when they are forced to walk blindly in the dark.

He did it for them nonetheless, however much they failed him. And he did it for us. He said 'yes'. He agreed to drink from the most poisoned cup ever offered—because it was his Father's will.

❖

Father, we say it every day in the words of the prayer Jesus gave us: 'Your will be done on earth as it is in heaven.'

Help us to meditate on what this might mean for us if we really want to mean what we say—what it might mean not in general terms but for us personally. On that night in Gethsemane Jesus was not given any special heavenly help in bringing himself to a place of total obedience. We too need to look within ourselves to what you have already given us and find the courage to walk whatever road you ask us to walk, simply because it is your will.

THE FINAL CURTAIN

At midday the sky turned dark and stayed that way until three o'clock. Then about that time Jesus shouted, 'Eli, Eli, lema sabachthani?' which means, 'My God, my God, why have you forsaken me?' Some of the people standing there heard Jesus and said, 'He's calling for Elijah.' One of them at once ran and grabbed a sponge. He soaked it in wine, then put it on a stick and held it up to Jesus. Others said, 'Wait! Lets see if Elijah will come and save him.' Once again Jesus shouted, and then he died.

MATTHEW 27:45–50

Somehow it had to be this way, didn't it? Even the last and most tormented words that come from our Lord's lips are grotesquely misunderstood by the watching crowds. It's perhaps not surprising, as in Aramaic the name Elijah sounds like 'Eli' which means 'my God', but it is still blackly comic. The only positive thing I can find to say is that I would doubt whether, at this moment, either Jesus or his mother and his best friend were even aware of the disappointed crowd that had been greedily anticpating a better finale to the show than this.

I have often wondered whether it was worse for Mary or for Jesus during those three endless hours when he hung on that cross. I feel I can now understand a little of what she went through. I have mentioned elsewhere that, at the time of writing, my mother is slowly succumbing to cancer. She is living with us—or rather dying with us. The cancer eats the nourishment I manage to get into her skeletal frame. I am watching her body gradually giving up its strength to the darkness that is engulfing her. One day soon it will devour her. Only then will she be able to go home to her Father where, I can't help thinking, a rather 'des res' is awaiting her. But first she has to go through the narrow door of death.

We stand as helpless as Mary at the foot of the cross, knowing that there is nothing we can do to stop the process and that all we can do is to be there. She doesn't deserve this. We long to be able to take some of her agony from her, but we are helpless. She hangs bravely on her cross. She forgives and loves and worries about her grandchildren's lives and continues to pray for all of us. She hasn't once questioned why it should be happening to her. She weeps occasionally, but not once has she complained or got angry. In her dying she is her heavenly Father's daughter, and I am privileged to witness it. I am so proud of her.

While Jesus is hanging on that horrible cross, he shows qualities demonstrating again and again that he is his heavenly Father's son, but he is also his mother's child, and however much Mary must have longed to take his pain from him, she must have been so proud of him.

No longer under his self-imposed rule of silence, he is again mediating on our behalf, as he did constantly while he walked on the earth. In the words 'Father, forgive these people! They don't know not what they're doing' (Luke 23:34), he binds in heaven what he has bound on earth, displaying that he still has the rights of sonship to claim forgiveness for those who are not even aware of their need to repent.

His compassion is as prominent a feature of his character as it ever was. He is still full of concern for those who cannot support themselves. Looking at his dear mother, he makes good and responsible provision for her future by giving her into John's care (John 19:27), knowing that as his mother she runs the risk of being hated and vilified.

He is still of the royal house of heaven. Faced with the faith of the thief hanging next to him, Jesus promises him a royal pardon and a place with him in paradise (Luke 23:42–43).

There is no sense of a dilution of confidence. Nailed to a cross in order to fulfil prophecy, bloodied and scarred and in physical agony, he is still Jesus, the Messiah, Son of his Father, on his way to receive back the glory that he had with the Father before the world began—that is, until those final moments when darkness takes control and, for a few seconds, Lucifer rules.

Then Jesus experiences the utter desolation of being in sin, the cord cut between him and heaven for the first, last and only time. He has become the sinner featured in the stories he told in the temple during the days before his arrest—'smashed to pieces', 'thrown outside into darkness', 'crying and gritting his teeth in pain', having the doors closed against him, knowing what it is to be 'punished for ever'.

At this point we suspect that nothing—nothing—has ever been as terrible as this. Our grief at my mother's parting, and Mary's desperate sadness, are as a single tear compared to the apocalyptic grief of Jesus and his Father at this moment. He must have known that it was going to have to happen, but could even he have prepared himself not only to be merely man but also to hold our sin in his perfect soul?

Stripped of this last vestige of his godly nature, totally enveloped in the final agony, the price for our sins is at last paid in full. 'Everything is done!' he cries (John 19:30), and Jesus walks out of this world through the narrowest of doors—the one marked 'EXIT'.

Jesus, you loved us this much and yet still there are crowds continuing to laugh at you, to demand silly miracles, to ignore you. Like the thief on the cross, we ask to be with you, knowing that we deserve nothing and owe you everything—yet also knowing that there is only one place we ever want to be, and that is with you in paradise.

EXIT

At once the curtain in the temple was torn in two from top to bottom. The earth shook, and the rocks split apart... The officer and the soldiers guarding Jesus felt the earthquake and saw everything else that happened. They were frightened and said, 'This man really was God's son!'

MATTHEW 27:51, 54

My father died when he was 96 years old. During the last year of his life, we witnessed the breaking down of both his body and his mind, so we could not be too sad for him.

We miss him, of course. All of us do. My mother, who had just six months living alone in their bungalow before she herself was taken ill, missed him greatly. We used to sit together, my mother and I, and remember the better times before Alzheimer's and cancer took hold.

One day, we were talking about the occasions when my father's father visited us and how good those visits were. Grandpa had been manager of a cotton mill in Clitheroe in Lancashire until it was closed down. As I was very small in the years when he was still well enough to visit us each summer, I remembered him especially for his fob watch which he would produce from his jacket pocket and let me flick open with my thumb as I perched on his soldierly knees. I remembered the hardness of his starched collars and the prickly bristle of his chin, which smelt of cleanness—and the walks he and I took through the woods at the bottom of our road to a small park. There he would annually renew his acquaintance with an elderly man who I was convinced must live in the park because he could always be found puffing his pipe on the cricket pavilion veranda. Grandpa and I called him the 'Cuckoo Man' because he could whistle that particular bird's call through his fingers.

My mother remembered one of Grandpa's early visits, when she tried to show him that even a young wife from south of the Humber/Wash divide knew how to launder handkerchiefs. Proudly she lifted the corner of one of the hankies with her wooden tongs, leaving the rest of it behind in the bowl where it had been left to soak, realizing with horror that pure bleach may have been a little too drastic to prove her point!

She remembered him for something else too. My father was a bank clerk all his working life, keeping very regular hours and arriving home at the same time every weekday. Every afternoon during his stay, Grandpa would station himself by our front bay window, fob watch in hand, waiting. Coming from a generation when it was believed that the husband, weary from daily toil, had a right to expect tea on the table as he walked through the door, Grandpa was convinced that my mother would rejoice in having a few minutes warning to complete her loving wifely tea duties.

'Kathleen, here comes our George. He's coming, he's coming, Kathleen,' would be the happy daily cry as my father dismounted from his sturdy old bike by the front gate, carefully removed his cycle clips and prepared to walk up our short drive. Excitement mounting to fever pitch in his wavering voice, the old man would continue, 'Kathleen, Kathleen, it's our George. He's coming in the gate now.'

I will not repeat to you the unedifying thoughts my mother tells me she sometimes entertained at these words, but I can say that the memory has never faded!

But what have these memories to do with the death and resurrection of Jesus? On the face of it, not a lot! These men of my family have little in common with Jesus. Neither my father nor my grandfather were young men cut off in the prime of life as Jesus had been. Their moderate, non-controversial lifestyles could never have provoked either attack or adulation resulting in an unjust execution. They were both good, sweet men but they were hardly world saviours.

The key lies for me in a short poem entitled 'What is Dying?' which I was given by a friend after my father's death. Apparently it has been read at memorial sevices for over a century but I had never come across it before. It is by Charles Brent, who served as the Senior Chaplain for the American armed forces in Europe during the First World War.

> *A ship sails*
> *And I stand watching*
> *Till she fades on the horizon,*
> *And someone says:*
> *'She is gone.'*
> *Gone where?*
> *Gone from my sight, that is all;*
> *She is just as large as when I saw her.*
> *The diminished size*
> *And total loss of sight is in me,*
> *Not in her.*
> *And just at the moment*
> *When someone says, 'She is gone'*
> *There are others*
> *Who are watching her coming*
> *And other voices take up the glad shout,*
> *'There she comes',*
> *And that is dying.*

What glorious hope and universal truth lie in these words—and what a particular image it conjures in my mind. I can see my dear grandfather in heaven, fob watch in hand, who has been watching and waiting for so many years to see his only son again. He is calling excitedly to his wife, my grandmother who died before I was born, 'Judith, Judith, it's our George. He's coming in the gate now.'

And what of another Father, longing for his beloved son to come home? The disciples, both men and women, had already known the saddest of days. They were still weeping for their loss. On this, the best of days, perhaps God called out proudly to his legions of angels and to all the company of heaven, 'It's our Jesus. He's coming. Here he comes! He's coming in the gate now...'

ONWARD AND UPWARD

The Sabbath was over, and it was almost daybreak on Sunday when Mary Magdalene and the other Mary went to see the tomb. Suddenly a strong earthquake struck, and the Lord's angel came down from heaven. He rolled away the stone and sat on it... The angel said to the women, '... He isn't here! God has raised him to life, just as Jesus said he would. Come and see the place where his body was lying. Now hurry! Tell his disciples that he has been raised to life and is on his way to Galilee. Go there, and you will see him. That is what I came to tell you.' The women were frightened and yet very happy, as they hurried from the tomb and ran to tell his disciples.

MATTHEW 28:1–2, 5–8

The man who takes his cross and follows Christ will soon find that his direction is away from the sepulchre. Death is behind him and a joyous and increasing life before.

A.J. TOZER (*THE DIVINE CONQUEST*)

These words of Tozer, which we read at the very start of this book, are echoed in the actions of those followers of Jesus fortunate enough to meet him after he had risen from the dead—and there were so many of them recorded on that most wonderful of days, Easter Sunday. After the paralysis of the Friday and the enforced rest of the Saturday, Sunday is bursting with action.

There is still fear—of course there is. It's not every day you experience earthquakes and meet angels. There are doubts and questions for the more cautious. There is awe for those who actually met Jesus that day, and there is joy—joy and a growing bubbling certainty that everything is going to be all right, that he had said it would happen and it did, that he really was alive and they would meet again. Life, far from being over, is just beginning—life in abundance. The spring of joy that leapt to life inside that empty tomb affects everything in its path as a trickle becomes a stream that becomes a torrent, and begins to sweep away the debris of doubt and despair and replace it with sparkling living water.

We can never experience what the first disciples did, but if we have courage to follow Jesus wherever he leads us, we too can discover the truth that Tozer spoke of: 'That life which goes to the cross and loses itself there to rise again with Christ is a divine and deathless treasure.' Following him will never mean that we can avoid the hard times, but he will lead us through them and beyond. That is what he promised, and if he could keep the promise he made to his friends that after three days he would rise again, then surely we can entrust him with our lives.

I have been in too many church situations where there has been no room for the cross in our celebrations. True, when we first meet Jesus, and when we first encounter the Holy Spirit, and when we first experience the forgiveness of our Father, the joy and peace are beyond anything we could have anticipated. We are born again—children once more. Children become spoilt and miserable, though, if all they are given by their parents are treats for no reason, with no effort required, no challenges to overcome, no stretching of their capabilities.

Our heavenly Father is the best parent. He knows the danger that the well of joy can dry up if not fed from a spring of cost and commitment. He must watch some of our behaviour with sadness as we try to compensate without committing ourselves to following him. We clap harder, sing louder and wave our arms around more, but inside us is a loneliness we never thought to experience again since meeting our Saviour. The 'new cross' that A.J. Tozer speaks of will fail us in the end.

In the Gospel story, there are many people after the resurrection who experience the joy of meeting their Lord again. For most, though, their joy would be mixed with guilt and sadness that they let him down when he needed them most. They were simply not there at the foot of the cross, standing in the darkness alongside their suffering Lord. He will see that and forgive them. But on that first glittering morning he reserves the very best treat for those dear, loyal women who never left him. To witness his death was to experience the greatest sorrow. To be there at his resurrection was to experience the greatest joy.

❖

Father, forgive us for the times when we fail you, when we turn our backs and choose our own comfort and safety. We want to start again, to begin a new journey with you as our guide.

Today, help us to allow Jesus to rise again from the dead within our hearts. If we are paralysed by sorrow, let him enter into our grief. If we are deep down full of doubt, let us put our fingers into his wounds. If we have lost confidence in our value in your eyes, call us again to follow. If we have got hooked on the cross and lost our joy, lead us away from the sepulchre.

Help us to begin again.

JOURNEY'S END

Some insisted that the journey
Was a waste of hope and time
Better to embrace the darkness
Set apart for such a crime
Still they travelled onward, upward
Stumbled, staggered, rose and fell
Just to own one glimpse of heaven
In the sightless pits of hell
At the gates the angels waited
Menace burned in every eye
Then the ranks abruptly parted
As there rose a joyful cry
'Let them pass, these weary travellers
Every one my blood defends
Bring the best that heaven offers
These who killed me are my friends.'

ADRIAN PLASS

(FROM *WORDS FROM THE CROSS*)

QUESTIONS FOR GROUP DISCUSSION

My primary concern is that you do not treat this book as a manual containing answers. Apart from anything else, I think you will be disappointed! I prefer you to think of it as a sort of benevolent tin opener, offering access to thoughts and feelings that are contained within you. (I hope it won't open a can of worms!)

As you come together each week, it might be helpful to begin by sharing your initial reactions to any part of the week's readings. My own experience of sitting in groups, feeling blank, suggests that jotting down responses during the week is a good idea. This might trigger sufficient in-depth sharing, but if not, I include some questions to help promote discussion. They are not intended to be worked through one by one with the aim of agreeing on a 'right' answer; neither are they intended to be got through as quickly as possible before the 'real' talk begins over coffee. They will be useful only if you are determined as a group that each individual will have an opportunity to move on in his or her journey.

ASH WEDNESAY TO SATURDAY: THE DECISION TO FOLLOW

1. What image comes to your mind about the gate and the narrow way? How do you feel about the quality of your spiritual 'whiskers'? Have you ever felt that you have been asked to go through more than you could cope with ?
2. Did the idea of being addicted to an aspect of your lifestyle strike any chords?
3. What is it that most frightens you about following Christ wherever he leads? What are the prevailing winds that have shaped you—for good and for bad?

4. How do you react to Tozer's idea of the 'old' and 'new' cross?
5. Have you had an experience of saying 'yes' to an unknown future? How does this relate to saying 'yes' to God without knowing what the future will hold?

WEEK 1: CHILD ENOUGH TO FOLLOW MATURELY

1. Have you ever deliberately said 'no' to God, and turned back from a gate that you knew you were supposed to enter? (This might be something that appears to be quite insignificant, like writing a letter or making a phone call.)
2. What has been the cost for you of following Christ?
3. Which essential item do you feel you cannot do without when you go away? Have you ever had to cope without it? What 'cherished certainty' do you depend on in the same way?
4. What else do you think you need to abandon in order to 'travel light' as Jesus demanded?
5. Do you think you know God's voice? How have you learnt to recognize it? Why is it important that you do?
6. Which part of the reading about diet struck a chord? Why? What imbalances are in your diet, preventing you from being in good shape spiritually? What have you discovered to be essential for a healthy diet?
7. What is the state of your fuel tank at the moment? Do you feel you are running on empty, or that you have learnt how to be refuelled? What do you feel is the main ingredient of the fuel you run on?

WEEK 2: STAYING SAFE

1. How has the narrow way been depicted by those who have influenced your journey? Have you ever allowed yourself to

follow a leader even when you suspected them of being, at least, only partially sighted spiritually? What were the consequences?

2. What, from your experience, does 'growing up' mean in Christian terms?

3. Who or what is holding you back from following the Lord more closely? Is it circumstances, or temperament? Do you have difficulty entrusting those you love to God?

4. Who do you feel you are travelling with? Do you feel you are travelling alone? What can we do to break down barriers between us so that we depend more closely on each other? (This applies not just to individuals but also to denominations and churches.)

5. How deeply affected are we, as Christians, by 'spin'? Does it matter? Why or why not?

6. Have you had to get rid of a false image of God? Where have you found a true image? Is there a specific passage of scripture that you feel sums up the true God?

7. Have you ever been tempted off the 'straight and narrow' by those whom you valued? How can we stay safe from the temptation of the comfortable stroll?

WEEK 3: THEY SAID 'YES'

1. Which character did you most relate to and why?

2. Which other characters in the Bible have helped you to come closer to understanding what journeying with God means?

3. How do you feel about the unpredictability of your walk with God? Do you fear it or relish it? How can you support each other in facing unexpected choices?

4. Think for a while about Mary's choice to say 'yes' to God. What were the particular blessings that she received as the mother of Jesus, and what were the challenges?

WEEK 4: DITCHES, DARKNESS AND DISTRACTION

1. Who do we turn to when things go wrong? Have you ever hidden from God? How did he find you?
2. How much do you feel you actually rely on the Bible as a manual for living? Have you ever had the personal experience of the Holy Spirit illuminating the word for you? What else might help you to understand it in depth?
3. When the fog comes down, what do you rely on to make you feel OK? Are you someone who needs things to stay the same? What does remain unchangeable in your life, however badly you have lost your bearings?
4. Have there ever been times when you felt so close to God that you felt utterly safe? If so, where and when?
5. What has been your experience of 'stormy weather'? What special experiences did you have of God during that time? Or did you feel that he was far away?
6. What can you share together to help each other nurture forgiveness?
7. Have you ever discovered a way to inject new life into your daily walk? How much importance should we give to the creative gifts, as individuals and as churches?

WEEK 5: FOOD AND REST FOR WEARY TRAVELLERS

1. Do you find it easy to stop? What happens to you when you try to take time out with God? Is it important?
2. Do you feel threatened or encouraged by the idea that God knows us through and through? How important is the idea that he sees us when we try our best and when we fail?
3. How real are we with God? Do we edit our communication? Why? Does it matter?

4. Can we really change? Looking back, what areas of your behaviour have been altered since you first knew Jesus? Who or what has brought about those changes?

5. How much can we believe that our sins are swept away once we have confessed? How good are we at giving ourselves and others the same fresh start?

6. What is most likely to cause us to deny our friendship with Jesus? Has it ever happened to you? How did you recover your relationship?

7. This may not be easy to talk about, but do you have people really close to you that appear far away from God at the moment? How easy is it to entrust them to his care and to believe he still loves them?

HOLY WEEK: THE NARROWEST RAVINE

1. What is your overall response to the idea that Jesus deliberately set about creating the circumstances that led to his death? (Do feel free to disagree with this idea.)

2. At which point do you feel he made his hardest decision to move forward?

3. Do you think it is true that we need to be at the cross in order to rejoice fully in the resurrection?